"When I see effective fathers in action, I am impressed with how many different ways there are to be good fathers. No one pattern stands out from all the others as a best way. Each pattern fits the man. But I see some definite commonalities, ways in which the lives of children must be touched with consistency—the father's use of words, the precedents he sets in daily instruction, the types of corrections he imposes in ambiguous situations, and the ways he himself lives."

In this book Gordon MacDonald shares six vital principles for effective parenting—principles that can revolutionize your home life and the future of your children.

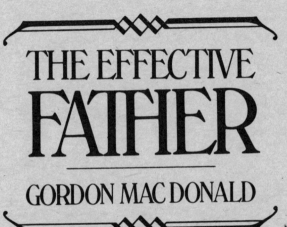

THE EFFECTIVE
FATHER

GORDON MAC DONALD

LIVING BOOKS
Tyndale House Publishers, Inc.
Wheaton, Illinois

Bible quotations in this book are taken from
The Living Bible or the Revised Standard Version.

Sixth printing, Living Books edition, June 1987

Library of Congress Catalog Card Number 76-58136
ISBN 0-8423-0680-3, trade paper; 0-8423-0669-2, Living Books edition
Copyright © 1977 by Tyndale House Publishers, Inc., Wheaton, Illinois
Printed in the United States of America

*To Mark Gordon
and Kristen Cherie who,
along with Gail, my wife,
are the most important
human beings in my life.
They cause me to pray daily
that God will allow me
always to be an
effective father.*

CONTENTS

The Effective Father

is a book born in a counseling session. A young man I liked very much came to visit with me about his frustrations as a father. During the hour of our conversation, I kept wishing that I could refer him to a book which would set forth some basic principles of father-child relationships. I couldn't think of a single such book.

After he had shared with me the fact that his own father had taught him next to nothing about the facts of fatherhood, I realized that there was simply no place for this man to go to learn the rudiments of effective relationships with his children. Before he left, I promised to devise a simple checklist setting forth some guidelines. Later that evening I sat down with my dictation machine and began to record a series of miscellaneous thoughts which amounted to my opinion of how a man gives leadership to his family.

The next day I showed the typed copy to my wife, Gail, and we began to pencil in corrections and modifications. Additional thoughts came quickly, and before long we both knew that God had planted in my heart something too exciting to let go of. A few days later Gail said to me, "I'm going to give you a gift." Naturally, I was intrigued and asked what she had in mind. "Eight days. I'm going to give you eight days of our vacation. We'll drop out of sight at our cabin; I'll cook for you and protect your silence. I'll talk to you only when you speak first. You take the eight days and write the book."

I continued to gather information, people prayed for my discipline and insight, and finally the special eight-day gift came. The typewriter hardly stopped from sun-up to sunset, and what emerged was a first-draft manuscript of what we would later call *The Effective Father*.

When I now look back through the final draft, I see evidences of the Holy Spirit's work in my life. There are thoughts and observations which I know to be the product of his illuminating work. Laced through the pages I see experiences shared with me by friends and family through the years. Finally, I see there the memories of experiences with the two children God gave to Gail and me: Mark and Kristen.

Often I sat down and read various passages of the manuscript to them. I had to; it was their book as well as mine. Some accounts of our own family life are very private, and they had to decide with me whether or not they would allow certain painful incidents to be told outside our home.

I sense that their permission to be a part of this book is more than the childish desire for the romance of "being in a book." I think they have caught on to a genius of living that is important to both Gail and me. They see, as we do, that God often uses models to get his points across. Someone has to open up his life to others and say in various ways, "This is where I am struggling; here I fell flat into failure; here is something I've learned and from which I've profited."

I have spent many hours brooding on the risk of writing *The Effective Father.* I wrote it as a pastor and as a Christian man who is a father. I did not write as a psychologist, an expert in family dynamics, or as a sociologist. The experts will quickly observe that. But when a pastor takes a pen, he integrates the insights of the Bible, his experience with people, and his own life. I hope that the result lies somewhere between the superficial and the statistical. Perhaps there is identification rather than instruction, challenge rather than correction.

I would be less than candid if I did not confess my fear that some day my own children will reread this book, then look back and compare its principles with what they see as my failure. The older they grow, the more I see how easy it would be for me to end up labeling myself an ineffective father. That frightens me each time I think about it. But I am going to see this book through because I believe in what it teaches, and because I think many men need to realize that none of us is alone in this pursuit of being the kind of husbands and fathers that God wants and our wives and families need.

While this book is designed for the male reader, most of its comments are equally relevant for women. If I need to explain my desire to write mainly to fathers, the explanation would be that much of the current literature is directed to women; very little on the bookshelves is written by men to men. If there are women who wish to read along, I think they will profit by the principles which are applicable to their own parental experience.

I thank God for allowing me to be a pastor and a writer. I thank God for Gail, Mark, and Kristen, who released me to write this book. I'm thankful for Dianne Stephens, who typed the manuscript and helped sift out my mistakes. My staff of pastoral associates supported me in prayer, encouragement, and work-assistance in our church, Grace Chapel.

Behind the pages of this book is the strong affirmation of the entire Tyndale House editorial, production, and marketing family, who make it a real joy to have a writing ministry. I am proud to be a Tyndale author.

GORDON MACDONALD
Lexington, Massachusetts

"I Had Always Taught Our Children..."

WHEN GEORGE JAEGER took his three sons and an elderly grandfather out on the Atlantic Ocean for a fishing trip, he had no premonition of the horror that he would face in a matter of hours. Before he would step on shore again, Jaeger would watch each son and then his father die, victims of exhaustion and lungs filled with water.

The boat's engine had stalled in the late afternoon. While increasing winds whipped the sea into great waves, the boat rolled helpless in the water and then began to list dangerously. When it became apparent that they were sinking, the five Jaeger men put on the life vests, tied themselves together with a rope, and slipped into the water. It was 6:30 P.M. when the sinking craft disappeared and the swimmers set out to work their way toward shore.

Six-foot waves and a strong current made the swimming almost impossible. First one boy, and then another —and another . . . swallowed too much water. Helpless, George Jaeger watched his sons and then his father die. Eight hours later, he staggered onto the shore, still pulling the rope that bound the bodies of the other four to him.

"I realized they were all dead—my three boys and my father—but I guess I didn't want to accept it, so I kept swimming all night long," he said to reporters. "My youngest boy, Clifford, was the first to go. *I had always taught our children not to fear death* because it was being with Jesus Christ. Before he died I heard him say, 'I'd rather be with Jesus than go on fighting.' "

Performance under stress is one test of effective leadership. It may also be the proof of accomplishment when it comes to evaluating the quality of a father. In that awful Atlantic night, George Jaeger had a chance to see his three sons summon every ounce of the courage and self-control he had tried to build into them. The beautiful way they died said something about the kind of father George Jaeger had been for fifteen years.

Few fathers will have their leadership-effectiveness tested so dramatically or so suddenly. For most men, the test will come in small doses over a long period of living. But the test comes to all, and sooner or later the judgment is rendered.

The world knows many fathers; it knows fewer fathers who are truly family leaders. Almost any man can be a father if he is capable of participating in the conception of a child. But fatherhood is more than a biological function. It is also a process of what I call effective leadership. Inside the perimeters of the family, it is the father who is required to create delicate conditions in which a child grows to be a man or woman, to attain the fullness of all that human potential that God has designed. Where those conditions do not exist, growth is retarded, and human beings fall far short of the heavenly objectives.

Families without fathers who are effective leaders face constant trouble, just like other kinds of groups where leadership is in a vacuum. We have seen leaderless situations—all of us. An athletic team lacking a leader usually loses. The business with hazy lines of authority generally goes under. A crowd which hears no charismatic spokesman becomes a mob.

Not so that night in the water! In a matter of minutes George Jaeger had had to make some hard decisions. Darkness, high seas, and a leaking boat were his enemies. All five people in that dangerous situation required every bit of strength derived from the relationships they had forged over the years. There had to be maximum obedience and minimum panic. The boys performed—as they had been taught over the years in less intense experiences—to the moment in which they died. If the early years of leadership had been missing, that night on the ocean would have brought death much sooner, and it would have lacked dignity.

Take a hard look at most of the fathers you know today. How many of them are effective leaders? How many fathers are engaged in the process of artistically, purposefully molding a family through the fingers of leadership much as the sculptor shapes plaster or clay? The chances are that you know very few. Where might we search for some viable models of effective fathers?

The media offer a number of father images which might set the scene for our thinking. Take Dagwood

Bumsted, for example: inept, a little bit crazy, successful only because each day's comic episode manages to end before anything serious really goes wrong. Scratch Dagwood. TV's Archie Bunker sets another style. Filled with prejudices and petty irrelevancies, volatile Bunker is ready at any moment to blow up his world. If he offers leadership to his family, it is usually in the sense that they assume a position generally opposite to the one he holds. Erase Archie. But then there is John Walton: calm, wise, working hard to make ends meet, seldom caught unaware in any crisis that life might present. John's image may be worth a second look.

The Bumsted home is zany; the Bunkers find themselves in complete chaos. But the Waltons bring nostalgia and hope to us. Something tells us—the viewers—that everything is under control. And it is because John Walton has the large view. He knows how to call the shots.

The Bible also presents a view on effective fathers when it calls a married man the leader of his home. Both the Old and the New Testaments provide descriptions and commandments which leave no questions about who is to be the head of the home and family. To be sure, the responsibility for the growth of a family is equally shared with wife and mother. But in a unique sort of way, God calls upon the man to be the family's governor, its accountable representative to make sure that God's laws are being followed, that the people in that family have every opportunity to experience all that their Creator intends for them to be.

When family leadership is effective, there is a sense of order and poise. Perhaps that is why the Walton Family TV series awakens such response from its viewers. We crave the kind of teamwork, the depth of relationships, the awareness of personhood that the Waltons portray. We want it for ourselves, and that is not a selfish preoccupation. It is exactly what God wanted the family to be. And where there are men willing to pay the price to offer in-depth family leadership, the chances are that the Walton experience can be reproduced and enjoyed.

A glance around the neighborhood reveals the fact that the Walton-type families are in a tiny minority. The man down the street, for example, has the idea that being the head of the house means being the king of the castle. He expects his wife and kids to wait on him. His time is his own; nobody tells *him* what to do. If the kids have any lifelong memory of Dad, it will be the view of his back as he rushes out the door for his next hunting trip, a foursome at the golf course, or a meeting at the lodge to have a beer with his friends before the Thursday night bowling league.

On the other side of the street is a man who thinks that family leadership means dictator-like domination. He demands his own way in every situation. In conflict he must always be right; he can never be wrong. You'll know his family the minute you see them. They're the ones who appear to have lost interest in home, who look beaten and crushed. When you talk to the older children, you discover that they can't wait to leave home when they reach eighteen. Their mother has given up; she has no place to go. She has put her personality in neutral. There is no fight left in her.

The fellow in the yellow house wins the prize, however. He doesn't lead at all. In his house, therefore, the reigning condition is anarchy. Usually his wife—in a state of restlessness or frustration, knowing that something has to be done—frantically takes over. Thus, his children are insecure and unfulfilled. He waffles on decisions, goes back on his word, and heads for the office whenever the homeside situation gets too hot to handle. There is a lot of sadness in this neighborhood.

A successful businessman invites me to lunch. He unfolds a sickening description of his family. Then he says, "You tell me that I'm supposed to be the head of my home. You challenge me to be a leader. I want to be the kind of man you are describing, but every time I try, I seem to fail. Is it because I don't understand what being a leader is all about? I guess my father was not much of a leader; perhaps I never had a chance to learn what was expected of me. What *is* an effective family leader anyway?"

Where does one begin to answer that kind of question, I ask myself? I've heard the same futile plea from too many men. The sadness of their quiet, yet desperate admission is made more poignant by the fact that it usually comes eight or ten years too late.

Another man—we'll call him John—stops in to see me at my office. Our conversation centers on his fourteen-year marriage to a "domineering" wife (his description) and his three children over whom he has no control (his assessment). He wrings his hands as he vents his rage over a woman who, he says, undermines his authority as leader in the home. He describes her as "closed-minded" in conflict, endlessly critical of everything he does at the church, and cynical about every dream he has for the future.

I ponder John's case against his wife. Perhaps I would feel more sorry for him if I hadn't learned a long time ago to listen first to the other side of the same story.

Enter John's wife a day later. She begins to share the struggles of the first eight years of marriage when the children were infants. John's prolonged absences from the home were devastating. After a twelve-hour working day, John would come home utterly exhausted, moody, irritable. If the children disturbed him, seeking some kind of permission or information, John would be too tired to respond. He would point them to their mother. But not so outside the home. John, his wife observes with a touch of bitterness, has been at one time or another the chairman of virtually every committee at the church and of the local Little League programs in the community. Chairman of everything, she says, but of his family.

Her quick tongue, her tendency to subvert his few directives, and her inclination to sneer at his promises are the result of too many years of nonperformance on the part of her husband. In the earlier years, when effective leadership was essential, John vacated the position, she says. Someone had to make plans and final decisions, and since John was disinterested, she did the job. Thus a wife formed habit patterns of authority-assertion and decision-making, far beyond the proper extent.

It isn't easy, she observes, to shake off the effects of fourteen years of one style of life. And she is right! John asks too much of his wife when he demands a new style of leadership. John and his wife are at an impasse. Having once abdicated his responsibilities, he will not find it a simple thing to reverse the roles that he and his wife play and to achieve a more normal relationship.

The symptoms of this fourteen-year-old family sickness are all over the house. The children, for example, have learned—as all children do—to exploit the cracks in the family leadership. Playing father against mother, they have perfected a system in which they know the precise time and the person to whom they can bring each issue and gain a favorable response.

John's daughter has learned that flattery and affection put her father in a mood in which he cannot resist any plea she makes for money, permission, or freedom from a responsibility. When John's wife learns what he has foolishly consented to, she is likely to reverse his decision. Crash! *Everyone* becomes distraught: the daughter because her plan is derailed, the wife because she is aghast at her husband's lack of wisdom, and John himself, because he feels challenged, betrayed, and ineffective.

Later I try to show John how these struggles over which he agonizes are not simply clashes of personality. Rather, they are the cumulative results of fourteen years of consecutive leadership mistakes. It took him that many years to get into this family mess; it may take a number of years to reverse the process. But he doesn't understand: John is sure that somewhere there is a "button" to push, a simple formula to apply, and everything can be all right in an instant. John cannot grasp the fact that there are definite principles of effective family leadership which have to be set in motion right at the beginning of family life.

"Why didn't someone tell me these things a long time ago?" John finally asks.

"Perhaps someone did," I respond, "but you may have not been willing to listen. It may be that chairmanships, sales graphs, and Dow Jones averages outpointed the job that needed to be done at home. Don't be too hard on a wife who had to learn to pounce on the balls you fumbled."

Whether the test happens out on the high seas or in the crunch of family struggle in the living room of a comfortable home, the time comes to count up the score. The results of leadership style emerge sooner or later. "I had always taught our children . . . " the head of the George Jaeger family says, and it showed, the night the pressure was applied. But then there's John: "Why didn't someone tell me?" Poor John!

1

"One Very Human Shortcoming"

Newsweek magazine told the story in a few terse paragraphs. If some of the words indicated dry statistics, others pointed up circumstances that evoke tears.

When West German industrialist Friedrich Flick died, he left a personal fortune estimated at 1.5 billion dollars, a business empire that embraced all or part of some 300 firms and a reputation as perhaps the crustiest, craftiest magnate ever to operate on the German business scene. Flick was dedicated wholly to his work (he buried his wife at 3 P.M. one day in 1966 and was back at his desk two hours later), but unlike such German industrialists as Alfred Krupp, Robert Bosch, and Ernst von Siemens, he never really made anything; he simply put companies together. "He always made the right moves," summed up one awed observer. "He was the Bobby Fischer of the industrialist world."

At his death, the Flick empire generated annual sales in excess of $3 billion. But for all his enormous power and wealth, *the old man had one very human shortcoming: he could not control his family.* By last week a Flick family fight over *der alter* Herr's empire had employees, bankers and politicians alike shuddering over the eventual impact it might have on the West German economy.[1]

Herr Flick's dilemma is dramatic. He could "put companies together," but he couldn't mold his family together. Like the powerless horses and men of Humpty Dumpty's poem, all the experts were having a struggle coping with the broken pieces left behind by Flick's failure as a father. What a human shortcoming!

Flick's faults as a family man set out a pertinent point, and it's this: success in one area of life does not guarantee effectiveness as a father at home. Flick scored at the office and struck out at home.

Herr Flick is not unique. Athletes have broken records on the field and had broken families at home. Churchmen have molded high-octane programs together, increased attendances, preached spellbinding sermons, but their ecclesiastical performance was a stained-glass failure at home. In short, being an effective head of a home is a unique, top-priority, challenging venture. We had better discern what it is all about and why Flick fouled out.

Someone asks for a definition for family leader or headship of the home. They want something in twenty-five words or less and I struggle to deliver. Finally I shoot back, "Define for me a quarterback. Where might one begin? Do you wish to talk about leadership charisma? Snap decision-making ability? Fast eyes? Strong arm? Capacity to scramble? Or shall we give a legal description: his position on the field, the limits in which he can move, and the things he can and cannot do. Twenty-five hundred words maybe."

Perhaps the place to begin a definition of effective leadership is with the recognition that there is need for order in family relationships before God and the surrounding community. People living in proximity to one another have to be placed in some design or there will be conflict and chaos. Disordered families create disordered communities. Thus, God has sovereignly chosen one person in a family to create and maintain the needed order. There is both a positive and a negative thrust to this leadership.

In its positive sense, effective leadership is designed to bring people to maturity, to the ultimate reaches of their human potential. The leader searches out the conditions in which each person in his family can grow to be what God has made him to be. But in the negative perspective, effective leadership is the enforcement of order when there is unwillingness to fit into the process of relationships, an attitude that makes life miserable for everyone.

The head of the home—like the shepherd in Psalm 23—carries a kind of rod and staff: the staff for rescue and pointing direction, the rod for discipline and enforcement. When both are capably used, there is stability in relationships and steady process in growth. When both are unused or misused, there is drift and deterioration among the shepherd's sheep and the father's family.

If we are fully to understand the necessity of this rod

and staff function, we need to take a quick glance back at some of the earliest paragraphs in the Bible. In the first two chapters we have unfolded for us a picture of what life was like in the beginning.

In his original state, the Bible says, man was without sin. That is to say, he had nothing in his life that might be described as imperfection or spiritual sickness. He had an open relationship with God. His lot in life was one of discovering what God had made in the world. He was there to enjoy it, master it, and use it. The very act of discovery and mastery was pleasing and glorifying to God.

But the whole thing became derailed when man sinned. Relationship on every level was shattered. The first man fell into conflict with God, hiding from him in embarrassment and fear—in other words, guilt. He developed inner conflict, and the symptoms of an inner war—heartache, fear, worry, inner frustration—plagued him. He began to mix it up with those about him; a cruel competition sprang up. He blamed others for his misfortune. Life changed from one of basic discovery to one of domination, searching out only what was best for number one—me!

The word which seems to characterize all these ongoing relational ways which have been in motion ever since the Garden days is *rebellion*. From a relational person to a rebellious person: a bitter lifestyle and a disappointment to God. Unless those rebellious impulses are checked, there will only be exploitation and destruction. The name of the game will always be "king of the mountain." Few kings—many slaves.

We have rebellious impulses within us, and they must be restrained at all costs. A primary way in which that is done is through the structures of human community. The family is the best example. It laces people together through love, binding commitment, mutual need, and authority. In its balance of relationships, the rebellious instincts of each individual are modestly checked and various patterns of responsibility and positive behavior are developed. If the family is a group of human beings so tied together, it is the father who is the knot where the ends of the laces meet.

From the positive side of experience, the father is the head of a unit of people launched on an exploration of life and all the things God has placed in the world for us to discover and enjoy. From the negative side of experience, he is the one who quells natural rebellion and stops members of his family from hurting themselves and others. There is no greater privilege—or responsibility.

That may be where Herr Flick missed some basic facts. Fascinated with industrial dynamics, he lost sight of his role as a father. All his cash and charisma couldn't do what effective father leadership could have done. Management consultant Peter Drucker would have called Flick an effective executive, but the Bible would call him a failing father. Flick is not alone; he has many friends.

He has biblical friends, for example. Israel's greatest king could have shared some of the industrial magnate's misery. He too was an effective executive—in the palace, that is. He could compel a country to unite in vision. He could raise armies, command them, and lead them to astounding victories. He built cities and wrote insightful poetry, but he left behind a group of sons and daughters who turned against virtually everything he had stood for. The geopolitical division of the kingdom of Israel can be traced to David's failure inside his home. He had one very human shortcoming—to borrow a phrase: He wasn't an effective father.

Call it Operation Rod and Staff, or call it being the head of your home, but that is what an effective father is.

It seems so simple, but the tragedy is that you probably couldn't have drawn David into your confidence and convinced him that he was flunking out as a father. He wouldn't have listened. He was too busy building armies and avenues. He would have listened only when it was too late. If only he could have been told that there are some basic principles to being the head of your home. Who knows? Israel might have been pointed in a different direction. If someone ever tried to get to him about these family matters we do not know about it.

It has been said, "You may not be able to do anything about your ancestors, but you can do something about your descendants." And that's what I intend to do. Link arms with me, and together we'll think through the principles of effective family leadership.

FIRST PRINCIPLE

If I am an effective father . . .

it is because

I have deliberately set as one of my life's highest priorities the creation of conditions in my home that will stimulate my children to grow to their full human potential.

2

"It's Not a Phony War"

THE HISTORIANS called it "the phony war," a pause in the military action near the beginning of World War II in which neither side—the axis or the allies—employed much firepower against the other. Armies just sat in place and nations diplomatically scowled. Because there was so little action on the battle front, the civilians behind the lines were tempted to relax their sense of urgency. From their vantage point there seemed to be little reason for worry. But they were wrong; we now know that the phony war wasn't so phony. In fact, it was the lull before a storm called "blitzkrieg," a series of German lightning-like strikes both on the ground and in the air that virtually destroyed the allied war machine.

I think the phony-war mentality describes my state of mind the Saturday morning our son, Mark, was born. As I looked at his tiny body for the first time, it was impossible for me to believe that his life could actually be a prize over which various forces might fight for influence.

I had stayed at my wife's side through the natural delivery, and both of us had witnessed life's most spectacular event—the birth of a child. From Gail's body had emerged a healthy boy, and the two of us could not have felt more satisfaction—Gail, that she had witnessed the birth; me, that I had not fainted in the delivery room! Leaving the hospital an hour later to begin the long distance calls to scattered family members, I brooded about the mysterious business of being a father. I was hardly much more than a boy myself; what could I know about the demands of effective fatherhood? And how could I perceive the reality that there were movements, philosophies, varieties of hucksters and widget salesmen who would attempt to seduce Mark away from me and the style of life in which I believe.

In a way it was like a phony war—at least for the first two years. I think my protective instincts were probably dulled because there was little outside interference; Mark was all ours. The few outsiders who did spend time with our son were handpicked by his mother or myself. It was no problem therefore to provide a home where—like the one on the range—seldom was heard a discouraging word, or, for that matter, any kind of word that was abusive or destructive.

To be sure, there were early parental struggles, but they were the typical ones: matters of respect for authority and property, obedience (instant, not delayed), potty-training (in the twenty-third month), and truth-telling.

We were generally successful—given a margin for the sinful nature—in setting some patterns of relationships with which we were comfortable. Sheepishly, I confide to you my naïve and premature suspicion that this challenge of being a father wasn't so formidable after all.

But any experienced man could have told me that I was being mesmerized by the phony-war period of Mark's life. And they would have been right. I was hardly prepared for the "blitzkrieg" which smashed into our family, targeted right at our son. The lightning strikes came in increasing fury with the onset of neighborhood friends, school, television, and the general tone of a society which has more money and things than it knows how to control or profitably use. By the time Mark was five, I was a father with battle scars; I knew I had a real war on my hands.

And how does one cope with the real war? One element of our religious society decided that the best way to face the crippling onslaught is to stop the clock. Fathers built walls about their families, made cloisters of their communities. Progress was pronounced evil, and new styles of dress, transportation, education, and leisure were stamped unlawful. This pattern of life may offer protection from something, but I'm convinced that life behind those walls is not superior to that outside the walls.

Another more common pattern of response to outside threats to the family is the creation of unbending rules and rigid disciplines which may be as impenetrable as brick walls. From this perspective virtually everything in the world becomes suspect; there is little joy in anything. When I see people who have a rule book as thick as the phone book, I am reminded of the days of my childhood when my mother would take me into the children's department at Macy's. Just as I was set to launch my lustful promenade among the toys, my mother would sternly remind me: "Don't touch anything!" For children who live in a family where everything is oriented about rules, where everything is treated with a "don't touch," living in the world is a lot like my experience in the toy store. Just look and yearn, but don't touch; never enjoy!

I think wall-builders and rule-setters are excessive in their view of the world. But the opposite extreme may be just as dangerous. Here is a father who treats life in the world as if there were no evil. His permissive attitude sees no threats, levels no warnings, and expects no adverse consequences. "I want my son or daughter to have every opportunity there is," a father says. "Let them choose the beliefs and styles of life that best suit them."

Somewhere between these two polarized positions is a perspective that makes sense. Naturally, civilization isn't all evil, and the amount of reality in the world to discover and enjoy is mind-expanding. But the father who hasn't perceived that life in this age is much like crossing a mine field during a war, had better prepare himself for some heavy casualties. I recall seeing somewhere a war photograph showing a squad of men crossing a heavily mined field. At the point is a specialist carrying a mine detector. Some of the land is apparently safe, but other parts are salted with a lethal punch. Follow the leader, the photo says, and you will stay alive.

The apostle Paul bluntly warned the Ephesian Christians that life in the world could be a heavy battle. The enemy of one's spirit, he said, is not always visible. Rather, he is often invisible, fighting from ambushes which appear at first glance to be attractive and beneficial. St. Paul's advice: be prepared, alert, and equipped to stand firm. To the Corinthians he said that we should never be ignorant of the enemy's designs. Peter agreed in his epistle, and he described the enemy as one who is like a roaring lion, "seeking whom he may devour." These men weren't kidding around. Theirs was no paranoic fantasy. They were well aware that spiritual survival demands a dramatic effort.

The effective father also takes this kind of thing seriously, and he trains his eye to discriminate between those things that will build and those that will destroy his children's lives. He begins to notice repetitive hostile patterns in various areas of life which demand acute, sensitive awareness, lest from among the good things the destructive elements emerge that erode and tear at his children's spirits.

A spiritual mine detector might register a few things capable of exploding in a family's face. I began, for example, to notice that it takes an enormous amount of wisdom even to read the daily newspaper. Since the publisher has to print items which appeal to the majority of his readers, the columns tend to include large doses of subject matter about people our society considers glamorous and admirable. More frequently than not, therefore, the daily paper includes interviews and descriptions of men and women who boast of the so-called "free style." Last week a mainline article highlighted a New York Society woman who claimed a happy marriage in which outside "affairs" were fully known and approved of by her husband, who apparently enjoyed reciprocal privileges. The article is written in amoral terms, passing no judgment—perhaps even implying that if everyone could try it, we would all be emotionally much more healthy. In fact fidelity is equated with being "up tight." Hardly a week passes without some details about a Hollywood couple living together, raising children outside of marriage, and suggesting that others ought to try it. Remember, our children can read this stuff.

Sexual morals are not the only area where the newspaper sets a tone that says "Everybody's doing it; what's wrong with me?" The sports pages are constantly filled with a paralyzing spirit of vicious criticism of athletes who may have performed poorly on the field the day before or upon a coach who is to be made scapegoat for a losing streak. As a result, human beings are torn apart. We can't underestimate the insidious effect upon young people who are spectators to words which razor men to shreds, labeling them as "old" at age thirty-five, crying for their scalps because of a fumbled ball, and on the other hand, lionizing them when they break rules and escape the consequences. The whole mentality says something to the young family member who learns a new way of thinking and evaluation. Turn to the editorial pages; the same mind-set persists, only the attacks now zero in on politicians, educators, religious leaders.

Television picks up where the newspaper leaves off and enhances it all in living color when it enters our homes. Innocent comedy situations are but one example of the subtle deterioration in an overall view of human commitment. Mary Tyler Moore was a favorite in our family until the writers of the show—having captured our family's affection—decided that the story line needed a bit of "bluing." We began to see Mary in scenes which winked at basic moral concepts, and these increased in frequency. I guess what made it so bad was that the original Mary had created such a good taste in our mouths. But the new Mary faked us out: she won our loyalty, and now she is systematically betraying those of us who would like to laugh with our children at something wholesome.

An entire book would be inadequate to expose the subtle messages being sent over the airwaves to our families. Soap operas describe a trail of broken and twisted relationships; game shows communicate the idea that material objects are infinitely desirable and that lots and lots of things are free and come easily; violence of every variety tends to anesthetize our children—and ourselves —to the actual horror of suffering and death.

These are some of the ways the electronic and printed media create a battlefield upon which the effective father must fight. The answer does not lie in canceling the papers or banning the TV. That's been tried, and it doesn't work. The only answer is awareness and active participation in evaluating the alternatives and choosing healthy media input. What father who loves his family would permit just any unknown person to enter his home freely? In this age of communications his job as doorkeeper extends to those who enter through print and airwaves.

Many fathers face a second area of struggle, and it emerges from the world of industry. We call it the problem of the absent father. He is what the term implies: gone too much. We can't turn the clock backwards, but a quick glance at the father of the agricultural era might help us to see the mess we're in. The farm family worked together, and the father was on display for all to see. Children not only saw their father resting in the evening, if he got a chance, but they saw him performing under pressure and stress. If the cow kicked over a pail of milk, the kids were probably on hand to assess Dad's response. If a hailstorm wiped out the crop, they shared his grief. They were with him during the birth, the care and feeding, and the death of animals.

It was this constant family fellowship which molded the lifestyle of each child. But that constant presence simply doesn't exist any longer in most families. Since a father leaves home in the early morning hours, his productive role in the world, his personal reactions under stress, his most meaningful relationships are all hidden from his children. In those times when they could have learned most, he is absent from them. The leftover time in the day is usually marked by fatigue and staleness and the potential freshness of parent-child relationship is lost. In this new system of life that we have arranged for ourselves, intergenerational work can hardly exist. The resulting homelife tends to be leisure-oriented—home is the place where we all come to relax, eat, and sleep. (Everyone, that is, except the housewife.) The epicenter for creativity and productivity has been transferred from the home to the office, the school, and the marketplace. That can't help but diminish the significance of home.

Perhaps the most grotesque example of the absent father is the new breed of engineer, scientist, or military career man who works under conditions of strict national security. This father is not only absent in terms of time and place, but he is also absent in that his family does not have the slightest idea of what he does to make a living. Even as these words are written there are scores of submarines under the ocean which will remain there up to ninety days at a time. At home, children are completely ignorant—and always will be—as to what part of the world their sailor fathers are in at this moment, and their mothers know no more than they. The absent father creates high voltage tension in the home, forcing mothers to assume responsibilities which should not be theirs, and denies children the kind of exposure to their fathers that they desperately need.

I am thankful for public education, but as a father I have learned that this also is an area to be watched for potential conflict. Education as a major force in our society has long since washed over the original boundaries of scholastic activity: reading, writing, and arithmetic. Spreading out over large areas of human interest, public education now offers a child experience in everything from sex instruction to career counseling, from theories of his personal origin to speculations about his destiny.

A father describes for me the total communications blackout between himself and his daughter. As we retrace the steps of their relationship, he says, "I suddenly realized that school activities had taken over her life. It was band practice at seven in the morning until class time, it was play practice until supper time, and then it was heavy-duty homework until midnight. I found it easy to allow her schedule to be occupied with everything else but time with me. In the meantime I pursued my own interests."

That is why if one accuses the educational world of over-extending its proper influence, educators could rightfully blame the neglectful family. One senses a competitive circle moving faster and faster, tighter and tighter. The more the family surrenders its children, the more the state is willing to step in and assume responsibility.

It was positively chilling to realize that I was giving my children into the hands of instructors whom I did not know personally. Five days each week and the best six or seven hours of each day belong to people with whom I am barely acquainted. By the very nature of things, their word, their opinions, their values are often law. Your children, like mine, will be bombarded with discussion, reading, thinking, and exploration from which the name of God will be carefully excluded. This is a cause for serious thought if a man believes that all reality, all matter, has a theistic basis.

The subtle force of an unrestrained educational influence began to dawn upon me when our daughter came home from a second-grade writing lesson. Gail was looking over her shoulder while she practiced certain writing exercises. When she began to correct the way Kristi was writing one particular letter, our seven-year-old turned with some impatience and said, "My teacher warned us that our parents wouldn't like the way we were writing this letter, but that we should do it *her* way anyhow." A small thing, to be sure. But it was the beginning of greater and greater issues in which our children can be taught that the thinking of the "system" is more significant than the thinking in the home. That makes me shiver.

If you're still walking the mine field with me, don't discount the effect of affluence. As material goods become more available, the need for relationships and inner personal strength wanes. I'd never quite caught the impact of that until one night I clashed with my son. I was about to exile him to his room and deny him the fellowship of the family for an evening, when suddenly it came to me that banishment wasn't quite the same thing it had been when I was a boy. Confined to his room, Mark could amuse himself with his radio, his cassette recorder, a telegraph set he was building, numerous books and games, and a chemistry set he'd received on his birthday. Not a bad evening, I thought. In fact, if that was exile, I just might join him.

A world which measures life in terms of quantity rather than quality is going to have an indelible effect upon the inner spirit of children. One man put it to me this way. "I have had a hard time figuring out what we can really pray for these days." He's right; few children in North America have ever had to pray down the next meal to the table. Few of them ever worry about having a coat; rather, they can luxuriate in concern about color and style. Most are ready to discard a perfectly usable piece of clothing if someone in some mysterious backroom on the lower East Side of New York says that a new fashion has outdated the old. The unsuspecting father can be shrewdly conned into keeping up with the Jones children if he does not implement a forceful doctrine of economic restraint.

The family structure can be jeopardized by another potential enemy: the peer culture. The structure of our society has isolated people by age groups for large blocks of time each day. The adolescent, for example, is separated from those who are younger than he and can lose all sense of responsibility for meaningful relationship. He has little contact—except on an adversary basis—with most adults. His interest is forced to the horizontal —to those who are his age. With them he finds a kind of human fulfillment, a special sympathy which springs from their feeling of parental oppression. Popularity becomes an issue based on frighteningly superficial criteria. Entire age-oriented cultures emerge, identified by dress styles, special vocabularies, and unique kinds of social protocol. Industries have grown up appealing to the tastes of peer cultures. Radio stations direct a format at one particular age grouping. The destructive force of the peer group has been felt by many a store owner near a high school who has been arbitrarily driven out of business because a group of students decided that patronizing that particular store was "out."

The stronger the horizontal relationships, the weaker the vertical family unit. The two cannot peacefully coexist. More than one family has coasted along with what the parents thought was a productive relational experience until a child or two reached middle adolescence. Suddenly—sometimes within weeks—breaks in communication occurred, new loyalties appeared, and a father and mother found themselves bewildered over the fact that their child seemed to be a new kind of human being. What happened?

"Would you believe that we never had an ounce of trouble with her?" a mother says. "Then September came and she started the ninth grade. I don't think it was more than a couple of weeks until we noticed a change in the way she wore her clothes, the ways she began to speak to her younger brother, and the kind of boys she indicated she admired. Every discussion degenerated into an argument; every weekend became a crisis over where she wanted to go and with whom she wished to spend her time. She just wore her father and me down. It was as if we were living with a different person." The description is not a rare one. Peer culture has had its divisive effect.

As a result I have no alternative but to bluntly call it a war. The prize is the inner spirit of my children, and the stakes are high. Arrayed against me are those who wish to extract money, loyalty, and the strong creative energy my son or daughter may have to give. In the eternal dimension, the prize is the soul of my children. I am not prepared to compromise or negotiate. Until my children are old and wise enough to distinguish their enemies from their friends, I hold the responsibility to conduct both a defense and an offense on their behalf, demonstrating all the time how and why it is done for their benefit.

It is not a phony war the effective father faces. It is often a jungle conflict fought with the stealth of a modern day "guerrilla" who appears in the day as an innocent friend, only to return in the night as a bitter and exploitative foe. My eyes return to the war photo of the squad's leader, mine detector in hand, leading the way. Behind him follow his men; they follow because he has the capacity to discern the safe path. There are no careless steps; mistakes are fatal.

3
I Accept
the Mandate

JOSEPH. Earthly father of Jesus. How much do we really know about him? Don't be too surprised when you discover after some reflection that we don't know very much. Joseph is a rather shadowy figure. What makes him larger than life in our minds is the fact that he is the man in the nativity scene and that he made three significant decisions—decisions that would crush a normal father's spirit. Each of those decisions centered on an essential aspect of what most men might think fatherhood is all about.

Ask a hundred men what first comes to their minds in

response to the word "fatherhood," and a large majority will probably think about the act of conception. But don't mention that to Joseph. He didn't have that privilege, according to Matthew. The Bible says Mary's pregnancy was initiated by the Holy Spirit.

Take a moment and think through the inner agony Joseph must have faced as he pondered the words of the angel in the dream. What evidence we have points to the fact that Joseph was not a vindictive or violent man. Before he became convinced that Mary's story was true, he resolved not to make a public spectacle out of her but to dissolve their engagement with as little fanfare as possible. But when Heaven did confirm her story to Joseph, he confidently accepted the role of being a father to a child not the product of his life-giving semen.

Don't talk to Joseph about planning your child's future either. In those days when most fathers had the privilege of naming their children, thus expressing some of their future designs for their offspring through the meaning of the name, Joseph lost out again. Heaven would take care of that too. "Joseph," the angel said, "you shall call his name Jesus, for he shall save his people from their sins." Name and career, out of Joseph's hands. If Joseph had any sensitivity to what was happening in the birth of Jesus, he would have known that he was raising a boy who was going to suffer and die in an ugly way. He was being called upon to be father to a boy against whom everyone, probably including some of Joseph's friends, would ultimately turn.

Don't mention choice of home and community to Joseph as a mark of fatherhood, either. The third great decision Joseph had to make was to spend the first few years of Jesus' life on the run. The angel again: "Go to Egypt, and stay there until I tell you. . . ." To Egypt Joseph went with his wife and child. Who wants to live in Egypt? The angel again: "Now you can return to Israel." Conception, career, and community (to put it simply)—all the things one might think are marks of effective fatherhood. But in Joseph's case they weren't. What is there left for Joseph to do?

The old saying "Like father, like son" may require a transposition when it comes to Joseph. How about, "Like son, like father"? We may not know a whole lot about Joseph, but one thing is sure. He was one of the Bible's most effective fathers. And you can't miss the fact that it is true because Joseph *was* like his son. The thing that made him effective was not the usual ingredients of fatherhood, as we've already illustrated, but rather, that Joseph had an ear turned toward Heaven. The point is this: when Heaven spoke and offered Joseph a mandate to be earthly father to the Son of God, he accepted. And having accepted it, he ran with it every inch of the way. Every place he turned, things were on a kind of wartime footing. In the agony of the inevitable scandal when the community found out that he was marrying a pregnant woman. On the obviously bitter trip southward from Nazareth to Bethlehem when he had to transport the full-term Mary over a hundred miles of crude road. Through the terror-stricken days when the paranoic power-clique in Jerusalem swooped down on Bethlehem and forced Joseph to flee to another country.

There is a quality in Joseph, the father of a boy of whom it is said:

> And Jesus grew in wisdom and in stature and in favor with both God and man (Luke 2:52).

Those words say as much for the father as they say of the maturing young boy who grew up in the nativity family. Joseph did not live to see Jesus in his full-orbed ministry.

But in that strange mystery of the God-man, Jesus Christ, we see traits which came as much from his earthly father as they came from his Heavenly father. Jesus' attitude toward his mother (indeed, for all women), his ability to mingle with all kinds of people, and his capable hands which could touch, heal, or build—all say something about his father. I defer to Joseph as an effective father. He knew the real essence of fatherhood: to accept the mandate of Heaven and forcefully create and sustain a family climate in which God's Spirit could do his sovereign work.

I have a strong hunch that Joseph is a model for all fathers. He is a comfort to the man who has adopted children; he is a companion to the man who feels that many of the circumstances that touch his family are totally out of his control. Joseph is telling us something; listen! He's saying that the effective father measures the dangers and opportunities, tunes an ear toward Heaven, and sets out every day to guarantee the proper conditions for children to grow up to mature adulthood, to be what God wants them to be. "When Joseph awoke . . . he did as the angel commanded." Everything else is of secondary importance.

What Joseph is illustrating is basic: there are fathers and there are "effective fathers." The first thing that separates them is the moment when they *consciously decide* that effective fatherhood is a preoccupying way of life. They accept a mandate from Heaven in much the same way Joseph did. They confront the issues, face the potential enemies, and hear the challenge. "All right, I will," they answer, and they assume a new lifestyle—that of a positive, aggressive pursuit of circumstances in which their family can hear and know the ways of the living God.

Moses recognized right at the beginning of Israel's life

as a nation that a key to national vitality would be effective fathers. He linked the great theological affirmations
about God with family life. When he gathered the people
together he told them this:

> Hear O Israel: The Lord our God is one Lord; and
> you shall love the Lord your God with all your
> heart, and with all your soul, and with all your
> might. And these words which I command you this
> day shall be upon your heart; and you shall *teach*
> them diligently to your children and shall *talk* of
> them when you *sit* in your house, and when you
> *walk* by the way, and when you *lie* down, and when
> you *rise*. And you shall bind them as a sign upon
> your hand, and they shall be as frontlets between
> your eyes. And you shall *write them* on the doorposts
> and on your gates (Deuteronomy 6:4-9).

Moses is lining up with Joseph. Effective fatherhood
has something to do with a way of life. Call it—according
to Moses' approach—saturation leadership. His counsel
to the fathers of Israel is threefold: love God, keep this
love a high profile priority in your own life, and bathe
every moment of your relationship with your kids in this
reality. If you read the words of Moses a second time, you
might be surprised at the lengths he went to make sure
that fathers saw that this was a twenty-four-hour-a-day
affair: sitting, walking, rising, and lying. "Bind them on
your hand" might even qualify as the contemporary
equivalent of tying a string around your finger. In other
words, don't forget!

Moses' view of the effective father fits Joseph's. The
challenge is in saturating the routine of normal living
with the plan and the presence of God. In short, insure
that life within your home is so positive, so appealing, so

fulfilling that all else in the outside world pales in contrast to what a child receives when he is with the family.

The two active dimensions to Moses' charge to Israel's fathers are "teach" and "talk." In line with the first word, Moses apparently feels that there are times when a father deliberately sits down with his kids and imparts factual information that they need to have. The family altar kind of thing.

The second word is *talk*. And that takes place in the context of the ordinary routine. I think Moses is telling the effective father to carry on a running commentary with his children about the "whys" and "wherefores" of each event during the day. When a situation arises that might normally pave the way for a blowup of temper, that's a time to point out to a child why self-control is important and how it is achieved (provided, of course, *you* have achieved it). A moment in which a financial decision has to be made may prove to be a "talking" time to point out the advantages of economic restraint, the determination of values and priorities, or the process of a sound judgment.

I like Moses' system: teach and talk. It beats the tendency to jam a handful of dry doctrinal principles into a child's mind and then stand by, helplessly hoping that when the crunch comes, he won't lose his faith.

Why did Moses feel constrained to speak so instructively? Frankly, Moses was perceptive. He saw what no one else saw yet: the spiritual dimensions of Canaan. He realized that the moment the Hebrew people crossed into the promised land of milk and honey, there were going to be a series of spirit-crushing conflicts. It would be a land of sudden affluence and lush productivity. There would also be competitive religious systems. Add to that a population of seductive women, alternative ten-commandment-free lifestyles, and you have a scene set for some heavy challenges to Judeo convictions. Moses knew that what looked good on the surface would be destructive if one's guard was down. So, Moses issues the prophetic warning. Fathers, prepare your children while the going is good. It may seem like a phony war now, but there's a blitzkrieg coming tomorrow.

Unfortunately, succeeding generations of Hebrew fathers didn't take Moses seriously enough. You could have predicted it right there. The blitzkrieg virtually did Israel in.

Later, the writer of Proverbs would repeat Moses' approach to effective fatherhood.

> When I was a son with my father, tender, the only one in the sight of my mother, he taught me, and said to me, "Let your heart hold fast my words; keep my commandments and live; do not forget, and do not turn away from the words of my mouth" (Proverbs 4:3-4).

It is a wartime strategy, and it works. But it demands a general, someone who—like Joseph—sees the real issues of fatherhood, and senses the genuine dangers which stalk the inner spirits of our children and prepares to do aggressive battle. The effective father accepts that mandate. And it's time to say that everything in the rest of this book is meaningless if the reader does not consciously accept the same challenge.

4

Is There a Price to Pay?

MOSES laid effective fatherhood on the line to the fathers of Israel; centuries later, Joseph championed the pattern in the home of his son, Jesus. Where is the one who has picked up Moses' challenge and walked in the steps of Joseph? I cannot think of a man who would not like to be that kind of effective father. But my sad observation is that while many covet the title, few ever possess it. Why? Probably because few wish to pay the price which the mandate of effective fatherhood demands. It's just too high for the tastes and disciplines of most men.

We've all heard the story of some person who is offered

49

a chance to purchase a few shares in a tiny company with little more than a creative idea. There is a chance to invest the paltry sum of a few hundred dollars and in return gain possession of several dozen company shares. But the price is too high, the potential investor says; the risk is too great, so the opportunity is passed up. What about the company? The idea catches fire, and after a beginning struggle, it begins to sell products. Before one knows what has happened, the little company that started on a shoestring is grossing millions in annual income. Someone always computes what the investor who originally turned down an opportunity to buy shares would have been worth if the decision had been positive. The calculations show he would be worth untold millions of dollars now. But he isn't! When the opportunity was embryonic, the price was too high.

As a man aspiring to be an effective father, I set that familiar story in my mind as the prototype of what it means to make an investment in children. Like the fledgling company, a child seems so small, nondescript, and easy to handle with minimum concern. It is simple for a young father to reason that there are more important things demanding his time: advanced degrees, a climb up the corporate ladder, and lots of fun while one is still young.

What the imperceptive young father does not see is that the time to make family investments is when the child is young. Big returns never happen in the future unless sizable investments are made in the present. But the price seems so high for so little immediate return.

St. Mark tells the story of a rich young man with political power. He came one day to see Jesus. There is no record that anyone tried to stop him from interrupting Jesus' schedule. Naturally; he was important. He was in the prime of life. Let him get to Jesus. That was apparently the reasoning of those around the Son of God. He came, and then he left, a man "sorrowful" because he couldn't make the required adjustments in his lifestyle. He couldn't bring himself to conform to the high-priced demands Jesus made on prospective disciples.

What sets that brief, on-the-spot visit off in contrast is the previous event. Mark tells the reader that earlier there had been an attempt to bring children to Jesus. When the children arrived, the disciples said, "No way!" The Lord is much too busy to squander his limited time on children, they thought. The only important people in the world, they reasoned, are the older people—the ones with brains, power, and "wherewithal."

But, Mark notes, Jesus rebuked the disciples. He stopped the clock and he took children on his knee and blessed them. He delayed his appointments with all those important-looking older folk, to play with the kids. What was Jesus demonstrating? Just this: the average person may consider investments of time and interest in young children too high a price to pay, but one who evaluates human beings from the long-term perspective knows there couldn't be a better use of one's time and energy. He who would be an effective father had better not miss the message Jesus is giving.

Is there a price to pay? Unquestionably! And it is paid right up front, at the beginning of a child's life; the returns come much later. It is this question of willingness to pay the price that brings most fathers to a kind of paternal waterloo—because if they think the price is too high, they are on their way to being the counterpart of the man who had a chance at a big thing and passed it up.

When I examine the price tag in my own life, in the pursuit of effective fatherhood, several things spring to my mind and I discover that the mastery of them is an everyday pursuit. I think effective fatherhood demands, first of all, the price of putting one's *personal discretionary freedoms* up for grabs. This is the area of my life where I choose leisure-time activity, lapse into certain habit patterns, employ favorite words and phrases, and evaluate people and things about me in informal conversation. As an effective father, I can't escape the fact that these things have to be submitted to the x-ray-like scrutiny of God, and they have to be measured in terms of their impact upon my children.

Take *time* as an example. There just isn't enough of it in the average week for me to have regularly planned recreation with all kinds of nonfamily friends and yet have premium experiences with my children. Effective fatherhood demands that time in huge hunks be available for my relationship with my children. I see illustrations of maximized time need quite frequently. A boy or girl hitting puberty sinks without warning into a sudden mood. The young adolescent lashes out at everything in his or her path; the reasoning is irrational, and stunned parents wonder what in the world is going on. They cannot get through to their son or daughter. Normally, the adult reaction is likely to be to get angry, frustrated, or both. Perhaps even some form of retaliatory punishment might be the parental response. But this is a time for *time*. If the effective father has committed large blocks of it to a bowling league, to moonlighting jobs, to several church boards, he may not have a chance to deal with moods in the correct way. Short on time, he has to deal hastily and forcibly with his child, and the situation doesn't call for force. It calls rather for a father who can wait for the right moment, take his child into a quiet room and slowly talk the situation through, giving affirmation and affection until the mood is leveled out. His child needs reassurance, and reassurance often comes through the use of our time. Most men don't have it to give; time is too expensive, and they don't want to "waste" large quantities of it on children. But don't forget that Jesus did.

"Dad watches violent TV programs; why can't I?" a child asks. There is no good answer for that one, the effective father realizes. And so he tries to evaluate his freedoms in the area of leisure time entertainment, and he sometimes makes personal sacrifices for the good of his children. Like a good coach, he *also* keeps the training rules. Most fathers won't do it; the price is too high.

"Dad says that word; why can't I?" Caught again! Right! No good answer. The price again. Too high? "Dad leaves his clothes on the floor; why do I have to pick mine up?" The price again. Too high? "Dad, if you're going sixty-five, and the sign says you're supposed to be going only fifty-five, isn't that breaking the law? I thought you said . . . " The price again. Does it begin to register why there are too few effective fathers? The price is painfully high.

When I evaluated the price tag of the effective father mandate, I discovered another dimension: I found that effective fathers have a different concept of real success in life.

Charlie, my neighbor, whose kids play with mine, suggests that we walk together while our children trick-or-treat on Halloween night. Charlie is a lifelong Catholic, and I am a lifelong Protestant. That means we have a few theological differences, but we share many more matters of agreement than disagreement. As we walk along, we talk about the plight of the contemporary man in industry. Charlie says something like this to me, "Let's face it, Gordon; you can't easily be a success with the family and a success in the business world. Something has to go. They've offered me a top job in our company's executive management team. But do you know what that requires? A hotline telephone on my night table at home. Dinner with the company president three or four times each week. Business breakfasts every morning. Frequent plane trips all over the country. Weekend conferences at the whim of the president. You make a lot of money, and you get a lot of privileges, but the fact remains: you can't be a company man and a family man. One of them suffers. I love Joan and the kids too much; I told them to keep the job and give it to someone else."

Maybe that's one reason why I like Charlie so much. He knows what's important. He's an effective father because he has shaped his concept of success around his family. It's a big price, but when payoff time comes, Charlie's going to have beautiful children, and the fellow who took the job Charlie turned down is going to have a lot of money. If my pastoral experience is reliable, the man with the cash is going to look at Charlie and say, "Man, I'd give any amount of money to have a family like yours."

Let me add another dimension to the price tag that I find on the mandate: *Submission to the hand of God upon my life.* To put it another way, the price is letting God shape me to be a man who belongs to him and his way of doing things. Frankly, that's a painful decision, because it calls for me to make commitments in my life which are not always convenient or popular.

My friend Phil, the doctor, is a busy man who, among other things, has to be at the hospital to make rounds seven days a week. He's up at five each morning, and he follows an exhausting schedule. But as long as I can remember, Phil has always been in prayer meeting, has taught Sunday school, and regularly attends the evening service of his church. He is convinced, he tells me, that God wants his family to be at the center of the larger family at church, so he has driven in a stake of conviction. Nothing short of death itself is going to stop him from delivering himself and his family at the doorstep of church at those times when he feels committed to the spiritual discipline of fellowship and worship. There are many reasons why Phil is an effective father, and accepting God's claims upon his life is one of them.

Submission to God means a more disciplined prayer life: opening up the windows of my life to let God speak to me about myself and my family, and sharing with him what I think of the situation in the home. There are times when God knocks me on my ear with a piercing awareness of some place where I've dropped the ball. Does it hurt! But then I remember the words of Dale Martin Stone, who said in part of a beautiful poem about the work of God in a man's life:[2]

> How He ruthlessly perfects
> whom He royally elects,
> how He hammers him,
> and hurts him,
> and with every blow converts him
> into trial shapes of clay,
> which only God understands.

The mandate that Joseph and Moses throw down is there to take up. But the initial investment is very high, and there are many attractive alternatives. Don't pick up that mandate unless you're willing to pay the price. It's a big one, and it is the reason why there are so few effective fathers.

SECOND PRINCIPLE

If I am an effective father . . .

it is because

I have devoted myself to become an instrument and model of human experience to my children.

5

Setting the Pace;
Beating
the Tempo

MOST AUTO RACING appears to me to be carnage on wheels. But I must confess to an annual habit of tuning in on Memorial Day to find out who the winner is at Indianapolis. The race begins with a pace-car, a beautiful new automobile especially chosen each year to get out in front of the high-powered racers and lead them around the track for a few laps. The pace-car guarantees that every race driver receives a fair chance, that everyone is in his proper position and moving at a uniform speed when the green starting flag is dropped. At the moment the pack of race cars is properly positioned, the pacer gets out of the way—fast.

I also enjoy concerts. People often pay high prices because of one man in the concert: the conductor. He enters to the applause of the audience. A hundred instruments are poised by a hundred tense musicians. Each player is prepared to make a special kind of musical response to his beat; each section will produce melodic lines and rhythmic patterns different from the others. It is the conductor who will weave all the differences together and insure that the orchestra keeps faith with the composer's intentions. He will establish a standard tempo and a standard volume. He will bring out the solo parts, insuring that the orchestra colors the background in just the right musical hues so that the soloist reaches the anticipated excellence. Without the conductor, the finest musicians and the most expensive instruments produce only inartistic chaos.

Like the race cars and the orchestra, a family needs someone to set the pace and the tempo. When the pace has been properly fixed, the pace-car gets out of the way; so does an effective father. When the tempo has been set and the soloist steps into the spotlight, the conductor gives him opportunity to perform; so does the father. Without the pace-car or the conductor, you have confusion. Without an effective father, a family struggles.

Families need effective leadership not only because individuals tend to be rebellious toward meaningful and costly relationships, but because lives desperately need to be shaped and prepared for the day when the faster and more serious race of life is on. To complete my illustration, childhood can be likened to that period when the race cars round the track time after time until the pace-car and the starter of the race agree that the drivers are prepared to compete.

If we are ready to assume and accept the fact that God has revealed in the Bible a design of life for people to live, then the father can see himself as the conductor who insures that musicians are following the composer's score—that they are conforming to the intentions of the one who wrote the music.

In biblical examples of effective fatherhood, one can plainly see family tempos which are set by the head of the home. Mordecai, the adoptive stepfather of the beautiful queen Esther, is a classic example. Little comments threaded through the book of Esther provide insight into Mordecai's awareness of his pacesetting role.

> *Every day* Mordecai walked in front of the harem *to learn* how Esther was and how she fared (Esther 2:11).

> Now Esther had not made known her kindred or her people, as Mordecai had charged her; *for Esther obeyed Mordecai just as when she was brought up by him* (Esther 2:20).

When the moment of truth came in Esther's life when she faced a decision as to whether or not she should enter the presence of her husband the king and confront him about certain political matters detrimental to the interests of her people, it was Mordecai who set the pace and struck the tempo that moved her to take a leap of heroism. After years and years of implanting valuable advice and counsel into Esther's life, the payoff came for Mordecai at this moment. She knew her stepfather to be trustworthy, a man whose finger was on the truth. She listened—as always—when he said:

> If you keep silence at such a time as this, relief and deliverance will rise for the Jews from another quarter, but you and your father's house will perish (Esther 4:14).

These verses and the story that hangs between them focus on a man who sets a demanding pace for Esther's courageous performance. He got positive response from her in the crisis moment because he had taught her the force and value of his wisdom in her early years. It was instinctive for Esther to listen and trust Mordecai in the same way an instrumentalist pins the success of his solo part on the conductor by playing in careful response to the director's beat.

What Mordecai effectively accomplished eluded another man who faced similar opportunities. This second experience of fatherhood ended in disaster. In a time of national anarchy, Eli, the priest at the tabernacle of Shiloh, came as close as anyone to enforcing moral order among the people. But somehow he didn't plan ahead, and his two sons began to betray every ideal for which Eli was thought to stand.

At a time when most men should have been turning the family business over to the offspring, Eli received a disquieting visit from an angelic messenger. His sons, he was told, were simply unfit to fill his priestly sandals at the tabernacle. Their years of apprenticeship were filled with moral corruption, graft, and exploitation. Face it, Eli—because you've avoided it until now—your boys have blighted everything that they've touched. The tabernacle leadership will have to go to other, cleaner hands. The country needs your two sons, but since they've chosen such a pattern of behavior, forget it!

Where did Eli go wrong? First Samuel, chapter two, may offer some clues:

> Now Eli was very old and *he heard* all that his sons were doing to all Israel, and how they lay with the women who served at the entrance to the tent of meeting. And he said to them, "Why do you do such

things? *For I hear* of your evil dealings from all the people. No, my sons; it is no good report I hear the people of the Lord spreading abroad. If a man sins against a man, God will mediate for him; but if a man sins against the Lord, who can intercede for him?" *But they would not listen to the voice of their father* (1 Samuel 2:22ff.).

Not only is the paragraph depressing, but the futility of Eli's relationship with his boys is even more remarkable when you set it in contrast with Mordecai and the responsiveness of his stepdaughter Esther. There are several things worth noticing in this tragic account.

First there is that verb *heard*—used twice. The verb should have been *to know*, but it wasn't. Why did Eli have to *hear* about his sons' lifestyle from outside sources? A pacesetter *knows* where the cars are, and the conductor *knows* the moment a musician is out of tempo or what instrument is not properly tuned. Why didn't Eli *know* when the family tempo slowed up at Shiloh? To make things worse, he appears to have faced his sons with this rebuke *only* when he was an old man and they were adults. In other words, he'd let this thing escape his control for years. No wonder the paragraph ends with the fact that the boys wouldn't listen to the voice of their father. Why should they? They hadn't listened before. Apparently there hadn't even been a voice. This was no time to start, as far as they were concerned.

The next paragraph records a visit from a special person who confronted Eli with the mess he was in. Eli is given a bit of history about how God appointed priests in the past and made sure that they would be well cared for, so they wouldn't have to worry about their own security. And then God asks through the messenger:

> Why then look with greedy eye at my sacrifices and my offerings which I commanded, and honor your sons above me by *fattening yourselves* upon the choicest parts of every offering of my people of Israel? (2:29).

Something leaks out of that statement: it appears that Eli did in fact set a pace of a kind—*the wrong one.* Apparently he often winked at little overages in the past, small bits of embezzlement when he himself was hungry. Here was Eli in earlier days, saying by his actions, "A little extra for myself won't hurt from time to time," and his sons picked up the idea and carried it to the logical extreme. Isn't it a bit ridiculous for Eli to stand before his sons when he is old and rebuke them for something he started through benign neglect of the rules in the first place?

The end of Eli's fatherhood is indicated in one further statement:

> Tell (Eli) that I am about to punish his house for ever, for the iniquity which he knew, because his sons were blaspheming God and *he did not restrain them* (3:13).

God is really saying that Eli knew all the time—at least, in his innermost being—what was going on, and did nothing about it. As an effective father, Eli is a loser.

A practical approach to the kind of pacesetting we're talking about may be through two words that marked Mordecai's relationship to Esther: *initiate* and *motivate.* The conductor gives a sweep of the baton and sustains the beat. That's what Mordecai did, and that is what all effective fathers do in their family experience. While initiation and motivation are not the exclusive prerogative of the father—a mother is certainly doing her share —it is the father's responsibility to insure that initiation and motivation are always taking place, setting a pace of behavior consonant with God's design of life and relationships. It is his to stand one day before the heavenly throne to report whether or not the family played according to the grand score of God's plan.

When I see effective fathers in action, I am impressed with how many different ways there are to be good fathers. No one pattern stands out from all the others as a best way. Each pattern fits the man. But despite the differences, I see some definite commonalities, ways in which the lives of children must be touched with consistency. The downbeats of the effective father come through his use of words, the precedents he sets in daily instruction, the types of corrections he imposes in ambiguous situations, and, simply, the ways he himself lives. They are worth our scrutiny.

6

A Fountain
of Life

THE FIRST WAY an effective father sets pace is by talking.
Don't forget Mordecai; it was his words to Esther which
packed firepower. Through a lifetime of relationship he
had demonstrated over and over again that he meant
what he said. In turn, Esther learned that when Mordecai
talked, the voice was worth listening to. Having heard,
she acted, and everyone scored: the king, Mordecai, Esther, the Jews, and God.

Words have an awesome impact. They can build, or
they can destroy. The impressions made by a father's
voice can set in motion an entire trend of life. He has the

opportunity to choose his words, but he cannot always control the consequences that his words create.

If a father is prone to lose his temper and to pour out uncontrolled spates of words which hit children in the line of fire, he may find himself living for a lifetime with a crushed son or daughter. Words which explode at an impressionable moment can shape an entire personality.

A forty-two-year-old man has allowed me to look into the inner recesses of his life and see what makes him what he is today: a man who is frantically working himself into exhaustion; one who spends every dime he makes for impressive artifacts of luxury and success; a volatile human being whose temper explodes at the slightest hint of disagreement or criticism. As we talk I ask Tom to tell me about his childhood.

At one impressionable point in boyhood, when my friend was apparently displeasing his father with the way he was doing a chore, his father said to him, "Tom, you will always be a bum. You're not going to amount to a thing; you're a bum!" Tom goes on to tell me that whenever he and his father had angry moments, the same prediction would be repeated until it burned its way into the boy's spirit so deeply that, like shrapnel embedded in flesh, the words could never be removed. Thirty years later, Tom still suffers from his father's verbal malpractice. They drive him day and night from a subconscious source to attempt to prove that his father was wrong. Ironically, even though Tom's father is dead, the habit patterns of Tom's inner life still maintain fever pitch to convince a dead father and a slightly unsure Tom that he is not a bum. Let anyone suggest to Tom that he is doing something wrong or that he is deficient in some aspect of his life, and hostility, defensiveness, and furious energy are unleashed to guard against what he senses is a resurrection of the old accusations from a thoughtless father who verbally set a wrong pace.

A father initiates action in his family through words, and he motivates continuous action through words. He gives leadership instructions, telling his children what he wishes them to be, to learn, or to do. The idea is not to sit like a sultan, giving orders that maintain his own comfort or leisure. Rather, he is to assume the role of family manager, using his perspective to bring the family experience to a level of productivity and maturity. When he talks with his children, he must keep a number of ground rules which control effective verbal communication.

For example, he must discover that talking with children demands a heavy-duty effort at *verbal clarity*. Somehow he has to find the words that convey to his kids exactly what he wants to say. If they do not understand him, the children's responses are going to be out of line with what he had in mind. Compare the subtle difference between these three statements when a father is trying to initiate action:

> "I want you to be in bed by nine o'clock."
> "I think you should be in bed by nine o'clock."
> "I'd appreciate it if you were in bed by nine o'clock."

A discerning pacesetter knows exactly which of these phrases will activate which children. The younger the child, the more direct the words need to be. The more mature the child, the softer the direction-giving. Eventually, of course, the time comes when the habit pattern is established and there need be no instruction at all. Instructions properly given to children have resulted in habits rightly implemented by adolescents.

Clarity and precision are not the hallmarks of many fathers in their verbal communication with children.

Among the more common faults is that of failing to choose concepts that are clear to a child. We must ask ourselves if the thing we are directing a child to do is actually capable of being accomplished—at least in the horizon of his world.

Young Bobby is asked to clean his room. "Come on, Bobby, get your room cleaned up; it's a mess!" Bobby putters around and takes thirty minutes to do what appears to be nothing, and his father keeps repeating the same demand, getting louder each time.

But Bobby has a rough time knowing what the standards of a clean room are. At what state of picking up will the room turn from the status of "a mess" to being "picked up"? That may be an easy conclusion for an adult father, but it will certainly be a puzzle for a four-year-old until he has developed a series of adult-like standards for himself. Whose criteria are going to be employed to determine whether the direction has been followed? His or his father's? Does Bobby have a clear picture of the exact specification of what a picked-up room is and what pleases the one who has pushed him into action?

None of us, especially Bobby, ever warms to a task when the objectives are ill-defined and perhaps beyond our ability to perform. Thus, clarity of verbal pacesetting in this situation demands at the outset a clear understanding of what a father wants done and what it will take to satisfy his concern. "Bobby, the way you've left your room is unacceptable to me. I want every book and toy put away in its place; I want your bed made exactly the way Mother has taught you; and I want your floor to be completely swept—even under the bed. Do you understand what I'm asking?"

A time limit is also important for young children, and it's part of the ground rules. Time, like words, means different things to different people. Time moves slowly for a child; it flies for an adult. Forgetting this, it is easy for a father to expect his children to regard the value of time just as he does. But in fact they do not.

When Mark and Kris were between three and four years of age we began to give them daily chores as part of family life. They were capable of emptying waste baskets, straightening towels in the bathroom, and putting all of their personal things in their place. The problem we had was not with clarity of directions; it was meeting certain time limits. Chores were to be done before breakfast. But because the children would sometimes be slower than usual, breakfast was put off later and later while we all but lost our patience trying to get the kids to finish their jobs.

The timer on the stove solved our problem. I gathered the kids together. I informed them that I was through raising my voice in order to scare them into action which they had put off. Each morning, I said, the timer would be set for thirty minutes. When it reached the zero mark and the bell sounded, job-time was over. During the half hour I was not going to speak about the jobs at all. At the zero mark we would sit down to eat. The timer was the judge; if the work was not complete, there would be a consequence: possibly an earlier bedtime at the end of the day. I never had to interpret time and deadline again. The stove timer took care of everything. The clock was ruthless, and the kids discovered that they could not ask it to be lenient, to slow down to accommodate their mood or whim. Like their parents who have to live according to certain requirements of the community, they also are structured into a kind of system. The clock is their judge.

We've talked about clarity in terms of concept and time; let me add another ground rule which fathers often violate and therefore render themselves ineffective: *cer-*

tainty of command. Are the sounds a father makes certain or uncertain?

Children become astute—outdone only by their older brothers and sisters—at making accurate assessments as to how much their father means when he says something. In the life of an ineffective father there are a lot of uncertain sounds—enormous differences between his words and his actual intentions.

"John, I want you to go to bed," a father says. John grunts but does not move. Four minutes later: "John, I told you to go to bed." John's grunt now turns into English: "All right, Dad." But this is a stalling tactic worked to perfection after years of experience. John hardly even breaks rhythm with what he is doing. He knows the *certain* sound has yet to come. Everything so far is *uncertain*, actually inoperative. *"John* (the voice of John's father is now raised several decibels in volume), *I said get to bed."* John now moves toward the bedroom. Why? Because John understands *noise levels*, not words. In John's home, *volume* is the scale of seriousness. Soft sounds are uncertain; loud ones mean business. If John is bold enough, he may have the temerity to say as he retires, "All right, you don't have to yell at me." But he knows and acts in a way that proves that his father does have to yell. That is the system of command John's father has inadvertently created.

John's sister, Karen, also has the communications system figured out. When her ineffective father says, "Karen, mother says that supper is ready; I'd appreciate it if you'd wash your hands," Karen gives a feminine version of her brother's grunt. A few minutes later, Karen's father becomes aware that she did not respond. "Karen, I thought (apparently even he is not so sure now) I told you to get your hands washed." If father's voice is angry enough, Karen may be on her way. But the odds are that she will not head for the bathroom yet. She has learned to wait for a special temperature of heat to be turned on. "*Karen* (this is Dad's third salvo), I'm going to count to ten, and if you aren't in there. . . . " The old counting method: it gives a child ten seconds before he has to respond with action. Somewhere between six and eight the heat is high enough for Karen to move. It was not a question of knowing what Dad wanted. Rather, it was a question of how seriously he wanted it.

Effective fathers practice *certain* sounds; they mean what they say. Delayed obedience is considered disobedience. This means that the effective father doesn't count to ten; he doesn't raise his voice; he doesn't repeat that which he is sure was heard the first time. The request is made once in clarity and in certainty. No one has any doubt as to what the response should be . . . the first time.

There is a part of every one of us not made of God that resists authority as long as possible. Instinctively, we find every loophole, every excuse there is to avoid the direction and speed of the pacesetter in family relationships. Children will drift from dead-center obedience just as long as a lazy father allows them to. Therefore an effective father is always evaluating the time it takes to get a response from a clear-cut signal. When he senses drift, he must immediately retune the relationship.

One such corrective that works quite well is to call a family meeting. "Children," a father says, "I have become increasingly aware that you are putting your mother and me off when we speak to you about something, and that you really don't give us your attention until we've shouted or given several warnings. I can't accept that! I don't plan to keep on shouting or repeating myself, and I know your mother doesn't either. I'm sure that you don't care for it any more than we do. So because we all probably agree on that, I'm going to suggest that we go back to the "first-time" system. In case anyone wonders, the rules for the first-time system are as follows: I'm going to say a thing *once;* if I'm sure you've heard and understood, I'll not repeat myself. If I see that there's no reaction to what I've said, there will be a consequence. Now do you all understand what I'm planning for us to do? Kevin, tell me what you think I've just said."

The first-time system is implemented, and when a test-case arrives—as it will—Dad performs just as he promised. Consequence! You can be sure that the family will be watching from the next room to see if their effective father meant what he said.

Another ground rule covers the matter of checking through and making sure that there has been response to a father's words. Pacesetting in the family is a disaster when fathers do not follow through in checking out the reaction to their requests and directions. The man who asks his children to play quietly, eat in a more orderly way, or wash their hands, or prepare for bed but overlooks the results when his words are ignored, is really *a dishonest father.* His statements are really indications of "wish" rather than "want" for the family's good. It doesn't take a child long to see that his father doesn't mean what he says; he doesn't bother to check up on the results of what he's asked of the children.

Is there any of us that hasn't at one time or another seen a father or mother who has lost control of an unruly child? They keep *telling* the child to quiet down, but they never reinforce the action. These are the same parents who will wonder in years to come why their children ignore them completely. It will probably never occur to them that the rebellious part of every human being establishes a pattern of listening only to those people who follow through, checking on the results of what they've initiated.

Add to the dishonest father the name of *the threatening father*. He thinks he is giving directions, but he unwittingly gives choices instead. And they are usually prefaced with the word *if:* "If you don't turn off the TV and get to your homework, I'll take the TV away for the next two days," the threatening father says. He doesn't know it, but he has confronted his child with a calculated decision. Experience may suggest that there is a fifty-fifty chance that Dad will remember his threat tomorrow; he'll probably be at a church meeting anyway. "I'll risk it," a child decides unconsciously, and he proceeds on a status quo basis.

His father never thought of his directive as a choice; he saw the second part of his statement to be a possible consequence. But his child saw it as an alternative. Threats are usually bluffs, and the shrewd child reads them as a pro quarterback reads defenses. To put it another way, he can calculate the odds of the threatened consequence better than Jimmy the Greek.

There will be times when a child will accept the consequences of the threat in order to get what he wanted in the first place. This will become particularly true as the son or daughter grows older. A typical threat, "If you're not home by 11:30 P.M., you'll be grounded for two weeks," may be translated into a choice at 11:15 P.M. when a teenager decides that what he or she is doing is so attractive and exciting that the promise of a two-week suspension is worth the gamble. At 12:15, when the homecoming happens, the father is faced with implementing a consequence that he may never have wanted to hand down at all—especially if the next two weeks include some activities the father actually wanted his son or daughter to experience.

The exploding father doesn't understand the ground rules of response either. He just blows up, spewing words in every direction. He's been inconvenienced, embarrassed, or he simply feels defeated because—to use the words of one TV comedian—"he don't get no respect." I overheard two boys talking in the church hallway the other day. One asked the other, "What's your old man going to say when Mr. Amsden tells him that you cut Sunday school class?" The second responded, "Oh, he'll get mad and tell me off, but he'll get over it pretty quick. I'm not too worried about him." Some children *are* worried. They reflect their concern with statements like, "My folks are going to kill me when they hear about this." But the attention has been mistakenly centered on the explosion, not the building process.

It is kind of sad to analyze these exchanges between young people and realize that what they're saying is that ineffective fathers have temper tantrums, little else. They are saying that if you can devise a way to weather the parental storm, you can pretty much get anything you really want. The exploding father isn't really enforcing a pace or beating a tempo that builds human beings in their performance of life; he's simply causing a mild inconvenience to a child who is growing up learning how to do exactly what he wants to do. He's telling his kids that he doesn't like what they're doing, but if they can stand the heat, it won't matter much what he likes or doesn't like.

Perhaps the saddest of all the uncertain sounds that come from fathers who are ineffective is the sound of silence. *The silent father* says nothing. If we could bring deficient fathers into court under charges of malfeasance in the business of pacesetting, the silent father would face the sternest charges.

A woman talks with me about her husband who is an athletic coach. On the playing field he is a man with superhuman capacities, running back and forth, urging his players with a booming voice, forcefully correcting their tiniest imperfections. He can affirm them with an enthusiasm heard for blocks.

His wife sobs as she describes his homecoming each evening: an exhausted, almost depressed man who makes his way through the door, flops on the couch with the evening newspaper, and is asleep within minutes. He rises only for supper, returning to the couch for an evening of television and beer-drinking. His personality takes on color only if friends who know something about sports come to visit, or if the assistant coaches and players drop by for a skull session on next week's game. In the meantime, three children are growing up, and he takes little interest in them. He is a sensational coach, but a silent father.

"Don't bug me. I don't care. Do what you want to do." They are the more familiar verbal sweeps of his fatherly baton. He avoids decisions, actually laughs if the children make wisecracks at their mother during dinner, and avoids with a groan any comment about their moral and spiritual development. Apparently he has come to the point in his life where anything not associated with football is meaningless.

When I get a chance to visit with the coach, I learn that he has never been interested in anything but sports. His father affirmed him and made him feel accepted only when he was engaged in some athletic endeavor. Therefore, he has developed the habit of thinking that nothing in life is worthwhile unless it is involved in playing on a team or coaching one. He thinks his wife is a strong woman. She wanted kids, he says; let her work with them until they're teenagers. He can cope with them then . . . if, I think to myself, they can throw a forward pass.

My friend the silent father may understand the ground rules on the athletic field, but he doesn't know the ground rules of effective fatherhood. He wouldn't be impressed at all if I warned him that he was laying a foundation for his children to hate sports, hate rules, hate men, and even hate him.

The dishonest father, the threatening father, the exploding father, and the silent father: what a quartet! I wonder which one Eli was? To be sure, you won't find Mordecai among them.

The writer of the Proverbs says, "The mouth of the righteous is a fountain of life . . . " (Proverbs 10:11). We can apply the principle of that proverb to the responsibility of the pacesetter as he launches his words to bring his family to maturity of mindset and lifestyle. Let his words always be a fountain of life—not a pit of destruction.

7
No Day Is
Ever Wasted

IT IS SAID of Boswell, the famous biographer of Samuel Johnson, that he often referred to a special day in his childhood when his father took him fishing. The day was fixed in his adult mind, and he often reflected upon many of the things his father had taught him in the course of their fishing experience together. After having heard of that particular excursion so often, it occurred to someone much later to check the journal that Boswell's father kept and determine what had been said about the fishing trip from the parental perspective. Turning to that date, the reader found only one sentence entered: "Gone fishing today with my son; a day wasted."

Few have ever heard of Boswell's father; many have heard of Boswell. But in spite of his relative obscurity, he must have managed to set a pace in his son's life which lasted for a lifetime and beyond. On one day alone he inlaid along the grain of his son's life ideas that would mark him long into his adulthood. What he did not only touched a boy's life, but it set in motion certain benefits that would affect the world of classical literature. Too bad that Boswell's father couldn't appreciate the significance of a fishing trip and the pacesetting that was going on even while worms were being squeezed on to hooks. No day is ever wasted in the life of an effective father.

Family life is an existential classroom; it lasts for about eighteen years. Within the classroom are children who are like large lumps of clay. The longer they live, the harder the clay will become unless the potter consciously sustains the molding process, keeping the clay pliable—"shapable." Each day the effective father stamps into the lives of his children words, attitudes, habits, and responses which one day will become automatic. It would be frightening if a father did not realize this fact. For teach he will—whether he is aware of it or not. Ironically, teaching can be done either through design or neglect. Teaching, conscious or unconscious, will make an indelible impression upon a child's personality and become part of a composite of future character performance. The weaknesses and flaws of the father will be passed on to the children in either case. So the questions confront us: do we teach to build or teach to cripple?

At this point of discussion about life in the family classroom, it seems wise to distinguish between *attitudes and values* and *abilities and performance*. The first pair are more often taught by lifestyle—something we'll look at later on. The second—*abilities and performance*—are more deliberately taught through positive planning of family experience. How does a child discover his or her abilities, gifts, and capacities and then put them to work?

One answer to that question might be to think about how many opportunities a father has to ask his children to assist him in family responsibilities. A bicycle needs to be repaired. There are at least three ways to approach the need: the *lazy* father postpones any action. The *busy* father typically grabs a few minutes, quickly runs the bike into the garage, turns a few screws and delivers it to his child with the job done. But the *wise* father adds a few minutes to his schedule and shows his child how to make the repair by sharing the work. He may have his patience tested, but the decision will pay off.

The wise father is perceptive; he knows that several things can be learned in the simple exercise of repairing a bicycle. Diagnosing the problem is something that can be learned, and so is the exercise of selecting the proper tools to use. A standard of excellence can be demonstrated as the repair job goes along—teaching the kids how to do more than a half-way job, bringing it to completion. Proper maintenance of both machine and tools can be taught when it comes time to clean things up. For some fathers, repairing a bicycle can be an hour wasted; not so for the effective father.

One day I watched an aircraft mechanic putting an engine together. We were not in the hangar of a major airline; we were in the Amazon jungle where Christian aviators fly across many miles of treacherous jungle to off-load missionaries and equipment at remote landing strips where they live among and serve Indians. As he torque-wrenched down the cylinder head, I asked him where he had developed enough interest in engines to come out to the jungle and service missionary planes.

"My father loved to tinker with engines," he started. "Every time I turned around he had me out in the garage fooling around with something he was trying to put together. I think he gave me a monkey-wrench instead of a rattle when I was born." Each day when missionary pilots put their bush planes into the air, they do so with confidence; they have a good mechanic, and he is the product of an effective father who was wise enough to turn his garage into a classroom.

Don't leave this idea of working with tools as an illustration without realizing that a father shouldn't restrict his teaching about home and engine maintenance to his sons. This is a place for daughters also. We can never foresee the circumstances in which a girl might find herself in which her knowledge of how to fix a faulty electric switch, replace a fuse, seat a new faucet washer, change a tire, or jump a faulty solenoid might get her out of serious trouble. Nor should a boy be untrained in general work about the house: laundry, cooking, cleaning.

The teaching process is enhanced through the delegation of responsibilities. Children are assigned tasks that can be reasonably carried through to completion. Actually, it is wise occasionally to give children projects that are just a bit beyond their normal grasp, something that will require mind-exercising problem solving. Frustration of a creative sort can be a mind-bender; a child needs it. Perceptive fathers may drop a hint now and then, but for the most part, there are times when we should leave our children on their own to surmount obstacles and develop the satisfaction of pleasing us without assistance.

There aren't many fathers who can master all skills and arts. That's why a man deliberately exposes his children to as many other kinds of men as possible. Tours of factories, art studios, business offices, and construction projects have tremendous value. They provide time together, learning experiences, and wholesome recreation. Across the spectrum of activity children begin to sense their own interests, and as they respond with enthusiasm, the discerning father makes a note to provide extra amounts of opportunity in that direction.

Sharing with children *how* things are done is not enough. Relationships in the context of work are important also. For example, teaching children about the meaning of lines of authority is a significant exercise. Our twelve- and nine-year-old decide to go out on the pond for a canoe ride. As I push them off, I remind both of them that the older one is the captain of the ship; what he says goes. I make sure that both of them understand this important rule of the high seas. Canoeing has certain dangers. Therefore, it is important, I say, that Mark recognize that he is in charge. If he says it is time to come in, that is the decision. Kris faces an experience in which she must accept her brother's authority and appeal to him if she has a certain desire. In the guise of summer fun, a lesson is taught: how to use authority and how to submit to it for the good of the ship and its passengers.

It's a shame that someone hadn't gotten to Boswell's father to impress upon him the fact that every experience in family life can be a teaching opportunity so that no day is considered wasted. It is to Mr. Boswell's credit that he did more in his ignorance than others do in a lifetime of striving. I wonder if he knew the value of the question "why?" Driving along with children, a teaching father engages his passengers in conversation with simple why-questions: "Why do you think they have put all those signs up? Why do you think the builder made the bridge like that?" What-questions are also valuable. "What makes that picture attractive? What does that cloud make you think about?" Add to your bag the how-questions. "How do you think people will react when they see that load of wrecked cars left in the open field? How do you think we could help that lady who looks sad?"

When children have been exposed to various capacities and methods, when they have responsibly carried out tasks delegated to them, when they have shown greater and greater ability to participate in family decision-making, the wise father insures that the challenge will never be relaxed. As children grow older they become more of an integral part of the family's "survival."

On long-distance trips, children can read the map and enjoy the satisfaction of giving directions. If mistakes are made, a few detours will point up the seriousness of shallow thinking and irresponsibility. Entertaining guests can be a chance to let children plan the menu, create innovative table decorations, and assist in serving.

Camping has provided many opportunities to divide significant family responsibilities in four ways. When the four of us tumble out of the canoe after a long run down river, each person knows what he must do first if the family is to have a decent meal, a dry sleeping location, and a private outdoor bathroom.

There is a further capacity which must be mastered in the classroom of the family. Call it the teachable moment. We rarely *create* them; rather, we *sense* them. The intellect of a child has doors like the entry ways of a building. A teachable moment happens when that door has, through some circumstance, been thrown open. Fathers learn that the signals of a teachable moment vary with each child. For some, the signal is seen in a wistful look on the face; for others, it begins with certain kinds of questions. Don't overlook the "captive-audience moments" at the table, in the car, and in the moments just before bedtime.

When the doors to a child's mind are open, he is probably ready for any kind of experience of learning his parents want him to have. When the doors are closed, teaching a child will be like trying to jam things through the crack at the bottom.

No one can ever predict the instant of a teachable moment; he can just train himself to take advantage of it when it comes. The father who makes it a point to put his children to bed and to pray with them will often find that those last moments are alive with potential conversations. A child is tired, not too anxious to be left alone, feeling especially tender and affectionate. I would never trade the marvelous moments Kris and I have shared lying side by side talking in the dark about matters of childhood interest. All the barriers are down. The teachable moment in Mark's life comes when I'm willing to sit at bedside and administer a back rub. If I'll keep rubbing, he'll keep on listening. We talk about theology, sex, struggles, fears, and almost anything else.

Teachable moments also come at times of need. Sickness, injury, pressure to finish some project for school, all provide extra special opportunities for closeness. When the doors are open, the effective father rushes to the entrance with the things a child needs to hear.

In his book *Creative Brooding*, Robert Raines records the letter of a runaway son.[3] When his parents tried to get him to come back and he refused, they asked him why. He wrote them a letter. In essence he was saying, "When I opened the doors to my life, you slammed yours shut."

Dear Folks:

Thank you for everything, but I am going to Chicago and try and start some kind of new life.

You asked me why I did those things and why I gave you so much trouble, and the answer is easy for me to give you, but I am wondering if you will understand.

Remember when I was about six or seven and I used to want you to just listen me? I remember all the nice things you gave me for Christmas and my birthday and I was really happy with the things —about a week—at the time I got the things, but the rest of the time during the year I really didn't want presents. I just wanted all the time for you to listen to me like I was somebody who felt things too, because I remember even when I was young I felt things. But you said you were busy.

Mom, you are a wonderful cook, and you have everything so clean and you were tired so much from doing all those things that made you busy; but, you know something, Mom? I would have liked crackers and peanut butter just as well if you had only sat down with me a while during the day and said to me: "Tell me all about it so I can maybe help you understand."

. . . I think that all the kids who are doing so many things that grownups are tearing out their hair worrying about are really looking for somebody that will have time to listen a few minutes and who really will treat them as they would a grownup who might be useful to them, you know—polite to them. If you folks had ever said to me "Pardon me," when you interrupted me, I'd have dropped dead.

If anybody asks you where I am, tell them I've gone looking for somebody with time because I've got a lot of things I want to talk about.

Love to all, Your son.

No, Mr. Boswell, there is never a day wasted: at the pond, in the garage, in the car, at bedside. Every home is a classroom, and every father is a teacher. The doors are opened more times than we think. But they won't stay open forever, and besides that, there are too many others anxious to get their feet across the threshold. If we won't enter at the teachable moment, someone else will.

8

Fragile: Handle with Care

IT HAPPENED one day at the beach, and even though the day was hot, I shivered at the implications of what I saw. An eight-year-old was getting a bit too enthusiastic with a group of five-year-olds in the water. He didn't know his own strength, and what started out as fun was now getting out of control. Moments passed and some of the protective parents up on the sand were getting uneasy. They kept intermittently staring at the father of the bigger child. Didn't he see what was going on? Couldn't he do something about it before someone got hurt? He had to see what was happening, but he ignored it. That is, until things became intolerable. Only then did the father spring into action.

Booming voice: "Robert, get out of the water this instant! Blast it, Robert, I'm sick and tired of the way you are acting. Look at what you've been doing down there. Can't you keep your hands off those children?"

The child—nervously glancing sideways to see how many others were taking in this tirade—offered a whimpering response, "But Daddy—"

"Don't talk back to me," the father responded, more loudly than before. "Don't you argue with me; I saw what you were doing, and I'm disgusted with you. Now you sit down on the sand here for the next half hour and see if it puts some sense in your head."

The humiliated child slumped to the hot beach, his fingers beginning to trace lines in the sand, and his eyes lowered so that they wouldn't meet those of the curious children back in the water. The father turned, picked up his beer, and resumed his conversation with those around him as if nothing had happened. But something had happened: a human being was crushed.

The key words were "I saw what you were doing. . . ." How long had the father seen what his son was doing? Why didn't he do something when he first saw the problem arising? At the earlier stage he could have made a gentle correction; no one would have been hurt. Why did he wait until the matter had reached crisis proportions? Now, instead of the fun continuing, everyone felt embarrassed or vengeful. The father matches his son's immaturity with his own.

"Fathers," St. Paul wrote, "do not provoke your children to anger, [like my man at the beach], but bring them up in the discipline and instruction of the Lord" (Ephesians 6:4). Too bad the man on the beach never read Paul. Discipline and instruction means that sometimes a father has to take corrective action with his children. But it also means that the correction be done in such a way that it builds or redirects. It does not devastate. It is "of the Lord."

The Bible calls corrective confrontation a *rebuke*, and it is the rebuke that stands between an ungodly act and its painful consequence. It is the last warning sign that is given when a person is headed in the wrong direction and will end up in the discard pile if he does not stop and turn around.

There are many examples of rebuke in the Bible. One of the first and most dramatic was a rebuke given by God himself. Cain, the firstborn son of Adam and Eve, had disobeyed God's instructions regarding the proper mode of sacrifice and worship. When Cain's disobedience was made more obvious by his brother's presentation of an offering that matched heavenly specifications, he began to seethe inside. The roots of murder were beginning to grow within him. The Bible says that "Cain was very angry and his countenance fell." That's simply a way of saying that Cain pouted and plotted ways in which he could vindicate his position.

God offered Cain one chance to defuse the act and the behind-the-scenes feeling. He rebuked him with a question and a statement.

> Why are you angry and why has your countenance fallen? If you do well, will you not be accepted? And if you do not do well, sin is lying at the door; its desire is for you, but you must master it (Genesis 4:6, 7).

All the fine points of healthy rebuking are here. The questions force Cain to face the effects of his sin and willfulness. The statement points out the dangers of the present trend of action and its consequence. Finally, God points out the alternative—the correct way. That is the rebuke of an effective Heavenly Father. Cain rejected the rebuke, the consequences set in, and Cain destroyed himself.

Rebukes uncover cover-ups, and that's what God did. He faced Cain down on his actions and feelings. He would not let actions remain unaccounted for, and he would not permit feelings to fester within the spirit.

Prophets were masters of rebuke, and some of the great scenes of the Old Testament involve prophets standing before kings and dumping reality right into the royal laps. When Nathan rebuked David, things were already far down the line, but David got the point, and he melted. Some consequences, however, were already in motion; at least, David repented. Ahab never did get Elijah's point; neither did Nebuchadnezzar when Daniel confronted him.

An effective father walks in the footsteps of the prophets; he is a "prophet-type" to his children, and as such, he must have a grasp on the proper standards of behavior that the Bible sets forth. He must be sensitized to violations, and he must be prepared to deal with them before the consequences set in.

A rebuke is a difficult thing to administer when it is done properly. It is not always received with joy on the part of the rebuked. Witness Cain. But imminent danger is ahead, and the warning has to be issued. A lighthouse says to the ship's captain, there are rocks over here. An airline omni-station informs the pilot that he is a few degrees off course. An "idiot-light" on the automobile dashboard tells the driver that he's moving with the emergency brake on.

But the operator of the lighthouse isn't trying to offend the captain of the ship; the omni-station isn't trying to embarrass the pilot; and the idiot-light (despite its name) isn't trying to anger the driver. In all three cases, the messages are for the principal good of the one who receives them. Normally, everyone—the captain, the pilot, and the driver—is actually glad to get the news. There would be disaster if they didn't get it.

Fathers sometimes get confused about rebukes. All too often, rebukes are launched out of vengeance and anger. A careful examination of my own rebukes tells me that a large number of them are not designed to build character into the lives of my kids; rather, they are designed to halt certain things which are momentarily inconvenient for me. Since I am bigger than they are, I can make my will supreme. Thus, I may speak sharply or in anger because *I* am irritable, or *I* am tired, or because *I want* some peace for myself. In fact my rebukes may not be rebukes at all; they may simply be adult temper tantrums, as I've noted before. As far as I'm concerned, that's all I saw on the beach that day. That's why the child was destroyed; he certainly wasn't built up.

Rebukes build, correct, and warn. "A rebuke goes deeper into a man of understanding than a hundred blows into a fool," the Proverbs writer says (17:10). If in fact we are sending rebukes that deep into our children, then we had better be extremely careful about the nature of those rebukes. Before the effort is made, the effective father will weigh the contents, circumstances, and consequences of what he is about to say. Can it wait to a more appropriate time? Is it launched from a platform of love, or is it merely a sign of vengeance or irritability? And finally, will it not only center on the bad behavior which is leading to disaster, but also on the proper behavior which should replace it?

Training our children to hear rebukes and act upon them is a major aspect of our fatherly relationship when our children are young. If we have convinced them that the rebuke doesn't threaten their standing before us, their dignity, and their right to make a new attempt at what they have in mind, they will learn the value of a constructive rebuke.

A ten-year-old boy dissects an old alarm clock in his father's shop. When Dad arrives home that night, he discovers his work bench littered with tools and alarm clock parts. Finding his son downstairs, he explodes, "Son, I'm sick and tired of finding my shop in such a mess when I come home at night. You're not responsible about these things; you're messy and you never finish anything. Don't you realize how expensive these tools are?" A series of outbursts like that may stifle the boy's curiosity, his desire to work in the shop, or his hunger to enter this aspect of his father's world at all.

It could have been a teachable moment, engendered through gentle rebuke. "Son, I'm delighted that you have had time to take a clock apart today. I'm anxious to hear what you learned about the clock. But what would you do if you had to use these tools right away for another job? Now it makes me excited to see you getting into something like this, and you know that most of the tools are there for you to use. But part of the way we do things here in the shop is never to use something without putting it back. In fact, the job is never done until all the tools are put away. Why don't you share with me what you did with the clock while you clean things up? I'll stay here with you until the job is done."

Curiosity is affirmed; the father's pleasure in the boy's interest in tools is highlighted; and the necessary lesson is learned. That's a gentle rebuke, and it was sure to build in the boy's life.

OK, I'll admit it! There are some rebukes that will be exercised in anger. And rightly so! There are times of injustice and mistreatment of other people and their property, and it happens right in the family. It is hard to think of anger expressed apart from a louder-than-usual voice. But it's worth trying. The anger can be expressed in words, and it should be expressed at the action—not at the person.

Let's make sure that we distinguish between rebuke and punishment. They are two different things. A rebuke is something that takes place in time to help a person avoid drastically paying for his sins. There is still time to stop the trend before it's too late. A father expresses his anger in rebuke by saying, "I cannot accept what you are doing. It is wrong, and it must not happen in this family. It is not the way we are going to do things." No threats; no punishment. Just a signal that there are rocks ahead; someone is off course.

When David was an old man, he paid dearly for his failure to understand the necessity and nature of loving rebukes. When it became obvious that he was not going to live much longer, a power struggle began among his sons. Adonijah, second in line, got the jump on everyone and mounted a rebellion against his father. The writer of the book of 1 Kings has a poignant comment about what made Adonijah the rebel that he was, and the writer laid it right at the feet of his father:

> His father had never at any time displeased him by asking, "Why have you done thus and so?" (1 Kings 1:6).

If one compares the thinking of Paul on rebukes (Ephesians 6:1) and what David didn't do, there is an interesting tension in which a loving warning is given. Paul's view: don't do it in such a way that it makes your child angry and unappreciative of you. David's view:

don't ever say anything that may upset or displease your son. David was dead wrong. Rebukes may displease and disappoint a child for a moment, but in the long run he will be built up and therefore thankful.

The place for rebukes is in private. Out in public the rebuke humiliates; witness my experience at the beach. Then, too, a rebuke is always aimed at the *behavior* of a child, not at the child. He does not have to be held up in front of his peer-group as a loser. What he needs is a quiet experience with his father in which he is informed of the destructive trends of his actions and the proper substitute.

Dr. Albert Siegel said recently in the Stanford *Observer*:

> When it comes to rearing children, every society is only 20 years away from barbarism. Twenty years is all we have to accomplish the task of civilizing the infants who are born into our midst each year. These savages know nothing of our language, our culture, our religion, our values, our customs of interpersonal relations. The infant is totally ignorant about communism, fascism, democracy, civil liberties, the rights of the minority as contrasted with the prerogatives of the majority, respect, decency, honesty, customs, conventions, and manners. *The barbarian must be tamed if civilization is to survive.*[4]

Call him a barbarian if you please, and in one sense you'll be right. But does that view mean that my rebukes must be stinging, sharp, and surgical as I try to tame the "barbarians" whose basic drive is a rebellious one? I must also remember that they are delicate human beings whom God has placed in our homes to receive training in the matrix of tender loving care. The label stamped upon packages that can easily break says, "Fragile: handle with care." The effective father sets out each day to administer correctives to the "barbarian." But he keeps in mind all the time that the barbarian is also fragile: his spirit, his self-image, his personhood must be handled with Christlike care.

9

Wear Shoes
You Want Filled

LOT was the nephew of Abraham, father of the Jewish nation. He may have had an eye for lush real estate, but he didn't have a hand on the essence of effective fatherhood. There were probably those who saw the disaster coming long before it did when Lot was tagging along behind his uncle on the crescent-shaped trip that took them from Ur of the Chaldees to Canaan, down to Egypt, and back to Canaan a second time. Little by little, gaining from Abraham's know-how and liquid assets, Lot began to amass a small fortune for himself. When he hit the big time, Lot was a self-confident man. It apparently didn't faze him when one day he and his uncle Abraham had to negotiate to dissolve their informal business relationship.

Abraham was the charitable man. But Lot was the wheeler-dealer, always looking for the fast break to more success. Given a chance, Lot agreed to a land division which deeded to him the lush, fertile valleys of the Jordan River as it opened out to the plain of Sodom and Gomorrah. Lot's friends would have pointed out his quick decision-making ability; he didn't have to think it over, pray about it, or weigh any particular moral factors in the deal. He just "lifted up his eyes" and took the land in with one broad sweep of his vision. No question about it, the plains and valleys were for him. Let Abraham watch his own business go downhill up there in the wild highlands. If his uncle was dumb enough to agree to a split like that, he must have thought, he was smart enough to take advantage of it.

Apparently, Lot made more money than was worth counting. His decision had been a good one—businesswise, that is. Familywise—not so good. It probably all began when Lot set up his tents with the front door facing the skyline of the beautiful city of Sodom. Perhaps Lot had enough religion in him to know that Sodom wasn't a choice place to park his family—so they would live some distance from it and look at it. "Look, but don't touch" may have been the motto. It's pure conjecture, but there's reason to suspect that the trouble started not with Lot, but with his wife and two daughters. For Lot, Sodom was only a good view; he was too busy building up the cattle business. But for his family, Sodom was a temptation. All day long they had time to look at it. We don't know when it happened, but suddenly when the book of Genesis picks up Lot's story after having dropped it for a page or two, Lot is right in the middle of Sodom's city life. He is not only living there, but he is obviously one of the town fathers. Lot always did go for the top of things.

Not only was Lot a man who sat at the gate—meaning he had clout in the community—but his daughters walked a fast step in the local society. They were now engaged to young men in the town. And that's when the roof fell in. Unknown to Lot, as far as we can see, God had been building up a case against Sodom and Gomorrah. He was ready to judge it. But he reached a compromise with Abraham, many miles to the north and west, that if his messengers could find ten righteous people in the city of Sodom, he would not destroy it. That was fair enough, Abraham must have thought. Lot's been over in that direction for some time. Having a family of four, he certainly would have had time to affect the lives of six more people in time to spare himself, his family, his assets, and the city. That's what Abraham thought!

Wrong, Abraham! Lot didn't have six more. In fact, he came close to not having even four. The story went this way. When God's messengers arrived in Sodom, they came to Lot's house. They were almost mobbed before they got settled down. Some town Lot lived in. They asked the key question, the one that would determine the future of the city, *"Have you anyone else here?"* This was Lot's chance to perform—to show the visitors, to show uncle Abraham, and to show God that life in Sodom had gone well. But it hadn't. At best, Lot could produce his wife, two daughters, and two sons-in-law, and even they were on the fence.

The Genesis account says that Lot went to his sons-in-law and told them that there was trouble ahead, that the city was doomed, and that they'd better evacuate while the going was possible. This is what the Bible says about their response:

But he seemed to his sons-in-law to be jesting
(Genesis 19:14).

The most serious moment in Lot's life turned out to
be a hysterically funny joke. And why not? What did they
have to go on when Lot tried to offer special leadership?
His lifestyle? The way he had lived in the past in Sodom?
He hadn't talked about these things before; why should
they be so excited when he suddenly raised these issues
now? Lot was no one to be talking about judgment; it
certainly hadn't marked his life before this. He must be
kidding!

Lot didn't do a whole lot better with his wife. She
managed to leave town, but her affection for the beautiful
city made her look back. Lot became an instant widower.
It would almost have been better if his daughters had
perished in the conflagration, because they did nothing
but betray their father for the rest of his life. They made
him miserable.

We've likened effective fatherhood to the setting of the
pace and the directing of an orchestral tempo. It is initiating and motivating a family into healthy action and relationships. It's done through words, through teaching,
through corrective rebuke, and finally, it is done through
lifestyle. Lot joins Eli in the hall of fame of ineffective
fathers on the basis of the way he lived. There was no one
to blame but himself for the way things turned out. He
started at the top, finished at the bottom. His family acted
in just the pattern that he lived. And when the heat was
on, they acted according to what they had seen in the old
Lot—not the new one.

Like it or not, a father makes impressions upon his
children with far more than words. His behavior, the
pattern of conduct in his own life becomes both docu-

mentation and justification for anything an offspring wishes to do.

Among the few effective father images we have in the Bible is the one St. Paul projected on his surrogate son-by-discipleship, Timothy. He'd found him up in the hills of what is now called Turkey. Timothy's parents permitted Paul to take their boy with him and for years the two men carried on a father-son relationship that culminated with Timothy's taking up the flag of ministry when Paul laid it down. Paul treated young Timothy exactly like a son. Toward the end of his life he recalls the basic pattern of their relationship:

> Now you have observed my teaching, my conduct, my aim in life, my faith, my patience, my love, my steadfastness, my persecutions, my sufferings, what befell me at Antioch, at Iconium, and at Lystra, what persecutions I endured . . . (2 Timothy 3:10-11).

When Paul tried to assess the impact he had had upon Timothy, he did not put words at the top of the list. Nor did he rehearse doctrinal truths or methods of ministry. Paul's priority is placed upon training through model lifestyle. Timothy, he writes, you've seen how I lived in all the ups and downs of reality. "*You have observed. . . .*"!

Children do observe. What do they see? The answer separates the effective from the ineffective fathers. The former takes note of the importance of exposure to his children—that every moment he is with them is a chance to make a positive impression for the purpose of character building and spirit development. But the latter doesn't see this. His view of the family is one of simply living together and finding the home to be little more than a meeting place in which to eat, sleep, and have a little fun.

In a previous chapter we talked about the importance of teaching to develop abilities and standards of performance. Now we concentrate mainly on the breeding of *attitudes* and *values*. More than any other way, this is done through the lifestyle of the effective father.

With the bulk of a father's time now spent away from the place called home, the model of the father is being replaced by the lifestyles of school teachers, recreation directors, and child-care personnel. More often than not, children are learning major value systems in life from the horizontal peer-culture. The vertical structure is not there in adequate increments of time or intensity to do the job.

Even more tragically, children are finding life-models on the television. The model now chosen and copied is a detective—crude, violent and amoral. Perhaps the model is the foolish caricatures in a favorite comedy situation. Worse yet, models arise out of the ugly "free-spirit" personalities of various stars who pride themselves on living beyond the bounds of ordinary restraint.

Wear shoes you want to be filled. The beauty of Daddy's little boy clomping down the stairs with a pair of his father's shoes on is a nostalgic one. Someday he will do more than simply fill two shoes; he will fill the shoes of a way of life that he has seen in his father. At best, the effective father will have fifteen years to set the style, and the first eight are the most important. After that—and I am already being generous—we can hope at best to make minor mid-course corrections.

The importance of modeling a lifestyle demands time and opportunity. Sometimes we have to create experiences that will jam the family together where learning can take place. For our family, canoe camping trips are a time for constant exposure. Camping offers a chance to face stress and inconvenience together. We can see each other in the best and worst of circumstances, and we have a chance to make measurements of each other's reactions.

To my chagrin, I recall a stormy night in Northern Canada when it appeared that our nylon tent might get either blown or washed down the hill. It was miserable. Cold, soaked, and hungry, I performed in less than admirable style. Later I had to apologize to my children for being irritable and snappy. It was a time when my children should have seen me patient and calm. But I wasn't. I was angry at something I couldn't control—the weather. Fortunately, there have been other times when my performance out in the bush was better.

Gail and I have often seen the importance of acting calmly for our children under stress at home, when, for example, there was an injury and everyone was panic-stricken. That is the time to pray under your breath and assume firm command. These images of action and response are the ones children remember the longest, and they become patterns of how they will act later on.

Family games—which I have generally detested, since I was always a loser—are a place where lifestyle can be modeled. It is important for children to see their parents both win and lose. At this point, I'd like to give them a chance to see me win. I have no business head for Monopoly; I am unsuccessful at conquering Life; and I always end up with the homely Old Maid.

Games provide experimental situations in which we can show our behavior under duress, our ability to be honest and considerate, and our attitude toward those who consistently win. A game equalizes everyone under a set of rules. Children climb to the level of their parents on the gameboard while parents descend to the level of children. (I still wish I could win more, though!)

In highlighting the use of games and the experience of camping, I've illustrated certain artificial situations in which our lifestyle can be displayed and studied. But the greater part of modeling which will take place happens each day in the home. In the flow of daily activities the kids are going to see some things which will etch their way into the spirit for future behavior patterns.

Take relationships as just one potential area of modeling. Children do not always learn in the schoolroom how to treat one another with dignity and affection. You can't diagram respect, forgiveness, or servanthood. It isn't found in any encyclopedia that I know of. It is observed and then put into motion.

The way in which an effective father relates to the children's mother is of incalculable significance. The children watch and are strangely warmed when they see Gail and me embrace and kiss one another. Something tells them that this is a sign of security: all is well in our home. Furthermore, they begin to formulate within their own hearts an understanding of how men treat their wives and how a wife will respond.

My son begins to learn that there are times of the month when a woman needs to be treated with extra-special tenderness and understanding. We may not understand all of her reactions, but she doesn't understand herself either. He watches and learns from me as he sees me go out of my way to help a bit more conscientiously during those times. And he doesn't fail to note the thankfulness and deepened admiration that is returned from wife to husband. He's learning from the model.

The children also watch us in our conflict. They observe our attempt to pick our way across the prickly field of disagreement, how we choose our words, how we express our disappointment in something the other one has done or thinks. They hear the words "I'm sorry," and "I forgive you," and they learn something about how they should treat other human beings. It will be obvious that I disagree with those who say *all* conflicts should be carried on in privacy. Perhaps that is right if there is a marriage where one or both partners cannot control their emotions. But when we face conflict which is always constructive, we can expose ourselves to our children. They need to learn how to exchange differing ideas and perspectives. Where better than from their parents? Sure, we're setting high goals for ourselves in those areas when we ask of ourselves to bare the bones of marriage relationships to our children. But do we have a choice in the matter? Not only do children hear what's being said; they also hear those things which are not said behind their backs. Most children are incredibly perceptive of the kind of marriage that exists in the home. Our only real option is to create a marriage relationship which can be exposed to the children's scrutiny and give them a healthy model to follow.

Since our children are quite normal, they also have their conflicts with one another. A show-stopper in our home has been this: do you two children want to see your mother and father carry on like that? Do you want us to yell at each other? Would you care to see what it's like?

One day Gail got a bit enthusiastic with this approach, and she turned around and started yelling at me, calling me names and pretending to hit me with her fists. The two children stood there in obvious shock. Then they began to cry, "Stop it; stop it!" They had never seen us raise our voices, call each other names, or swing at each other. Even the play-acting was too difficult to look at. Then we all began to laugh, and the kids were able to get a picture of what they looked like when they fell into that kind of routine. The rule in our house goes this way: we know you children will disagree on various things each day; we only ask that you try to disagree in the same way you see your father and mother do it. The reasoning works—about 30 percent of the time. Perhaps the percentage will increase with advancing maturity.

Affection and conflict are two ways in which children's lives are marked by parental relationship. The way a husband and wife *work* together is still another. For the effective father, the old traditions of division of house labor dissolve. By setting the pace, a father teaches his sons that no work is intrinsically masculine or feminine. Cleaning kitchens, making beds, helping with housecleaning are all matters that both male and female can and should do. The attitude of the father in this area is of paramount importance. The concept of teamwork is taught; going the extra mile when one senses that another is tired; volunteering to do things over and above normal expectations—these inculcate in the spirit of children a realization of the value of productive and helpful labor. And they do it because they saw it first in their father.

The sheer joy of living is caught in the precedent of lifestyle. Being able to laugh, being willing to participate in free-spirit kinds of fun are the greatest memories children will carry into the formula of their own relationship. The look on our children's faces the night Gail chased me around the house with an aerosol can of whipping cream was worth a lifetime. The touch football games which always set Mother and Mark against Kris and me, with an ice cream sundae riding on the outcome of the game, are going to make their mark in the children's concept of what joy relationships can reach when we work at them.

Bruce Larson writes in his book *The One and Only You*:

> I have a great friend down in Montgomery, Alabama, and a few years ago he told me an unforgettable story of a summer vacation he had planned for

his wife and children. He was unable to go himself because of business, but he helped them plan every day of a camping trip in the family station wagon from Montgomery all the way to California, up and down the West Coast, and then back to Montgomery.

He knew their route exactly and the precise time they would be crossing the Great Divide. So, my friend arranged to fly himself out to the nearest airport and hire a car and a driver to take him to a place which every car must pass. He sat by the side of the road several hours waiting for the sight of that familiar station wagon. When it came into view, he stepped out on the road and put his thumb out to hitchhike a ride with the family who assumed that he was 3,000 miles away.

I said to him, "Coleman, I'm surprised they didn't drive off the road in terror or drop dead of a heart attack. What an incredible story. Why did you go to all that trouble?"

"Well, Bruce," he said, "someday I'm going to be dead, and when that happens, I want my kids and my wife to say, 'You know, Dad was a lot of fun.' "

Wow, I thought. Here is a man whose whole game plan is to make fun and happiness for other people.

It made me wonder what my family will remember about me. I'm sure they will say, "Well, Dad was a nice guy but he sure worried a lot about putting out the lights and closing the windows and picking up around the house and cutting the grass." But I'd also like them to be able to say that dad was the guy who made life a lot of fun.[5]

If children can experience from their parents ways of doing things that demonstrate that they have drunk from the fountain of joy, their own pattern of living will be far healthier.

The shoes a father wears will be filled through his modeling of mutual experiences, through his relationships, and finally, through the things a father is himself.

Take a man's personal performance under stress. I have noted fathers who have an unyielding conviction about maintaining family devotions seven days per week, but who can dissolve in unrestrained anger because a neighbor's untreated dandelions blow seeds over the fence and onto the front lawn. What about the father who demands perfect attendance at Sunday school but loses all control of himself when someone cuts him off in a traffic flow? Which behavior pattern speaks louder? Which will be more remembered? Which is more liable to be copied?

We can never overcalculate the intense study of children when they see their father facing a crisis. How will he act when a flash flood puts six inches of water in the basement? What happens when the misguided hammer hits his thumb? And what of the moment when the umpire wrongly calls him out in the annual Sunday school picnic softball game? Each response under heat in daily living is worth ten thousand verbal statements of personal faith and morality.

Words, like actions under stress, also drive their way home. Perhaps that's why I noted in an earlier chapter than an effective father offers even his vocabulary and subject matter to God as a price to be paid for being able to take on the mandate.

I think of easy-come-easy-go words a father might use when, with friends, he evaluates the local police, the governor, or even the highest officers of our country. His tongue may run freely as he expresses his frustration over taxes, crime rates, bureaucracy, and the myriad of common conversations on the subject of government.

"Those dumb police," a father says as he drives along, "always trying to stop speeders with their radar; why don't they spend their time catching the people who are breaking into our homes?" Innocent (?) words, spoken in an unguarded moment, fill the child's ears, shaping the attitudes which will leap to the surface when as a young person that same child has a run-in with the police. All police are dumb; he heard his father say so. Now he knows it to be true.

"All of Washington is full of idiots, and the man in the White House is the biggest one of all." General words spoken by a father who really is saying, "My taxes are too high this year." But planted in the fertile minds of small children, they bear the fruit of anti-government opinion. Later, a father will wonder why his kids feel the way they do about their country.

Many homes are filled with unfortunate, critical words about neighbors, close friends, pastors, and other people in significant relationships to us. If parents worry about negative comments and attitudes, it is usually only because they hope that what they have said will not get back to the people who have been the subject of the conversation. But a father's toleration of such critical and negative talk, and, worse yet, his participation in it, simply goes further to breed similar thinking in his children as they grow older. Every word counts.

I see the pace car moving down the track, and I see the conductor sweeping his baton in a grand definition of the beat. Thirty-three cars move as one; one hundred musicians blend in concert. All eyes are on the setter of the pace, and they study the one who sustains the tempo. What he is, what he believes, what he thinks important will bring everyone to potential satisfaction. It is in that matrix that I see the father who wishes to be effective. He will set a pace and beat a tempo. And if he does it right, the family is well on its way to fulfillment.

The pace car gets out of the way, and the race is on. It has provided a smooth, disciplined transition to the race. The effective father has done the same. The conductor provides the conditions for the orchestra and soloist to play the score. So does the effective father. Could there be a greater responsibility? Could there be a greater satisfaction?

10
No Busy Signals Here

HE WAS a tiny tot in a cartoon, and everywhere he turned to find some attention in the family, he got the polite brushoff. Mother was too busy; Dad was preoccupied. In frustration he finally gave up. Looking straight out at the reader, he analyzed the family situation this way: "The story of my life is a busy signal."

Busy signals on the telephone rank near the top of my own personal list of ordinary, everyday irritants. That pulsating tone that fills the ear always seems to be an insult, and although I try hard not to, I sometimes take it personally that someone is not eagerly awaiting my call—and my call alone.

Some businesses, knowing that busy signals drive callers to their competitors, arrange to plug incoming calls into a tape recording that keeps reminding the callers that they're on "hold" and will be enthusiastically answered in a moment or two. Some others even switch the line over to the bland melodies by Muzak. But no matter how you look at it, someone at the other end of the line is too "busy" to talk right now.

Children hear frequent busy signals in homes where fathers are less than effective. No home is without some busy signals, of course. But we live in a day when many children are confronted with far too many messages from their fathers which amount to, "Don't bother me! I'm tied up!"

Leisure, appointments, deadlines, money, and other objects of adult interest seem to outpoint any conceivable concerns a "mere child" might have. The normal response when the concerns of a child conflict with those of an adult is to select the more "mature" use of one's time and attention. We reason: a child has plenty of time; he can always wait a while; put him on hold; give him the old busy signal. He'll understand.

Why is it then that the child doesn't understand? Why is it that when he has heard enough busy signals from the same person, he "dials" another number? There are a lot of fathers of teenagers asking that kind of question today.

Among the dimensions of effective fatherhood, we have to include the indispensable ingredient of *approachability*—that one can communicate with Dad without strenuous effort and that when he's engaged in family dialogue, he will be *open, responsive,* and *concerned.*

Approachability is no simple doctrine of fatherhood to be set forth glibly on paper. We will never adequately fulfill *all* the demands made upon us by our children; at best, we can only hope to reduce the number of busy signals we send.

Fresh in my own mind are the countless struggles I have when my own carefully planned schedule is endangered by the demands of my children. They seem to enjoy having me around, so they plot a daily plan for my life. They want to talk and share with me all sorts of "interesting" things that are on their minds. They want to include me in their games. They expect me to drop everything and sit down with them in front of the television to watch the weekly adventures of the men in *Emergency*. When I protest and try to beg off, Gail will devastate my defenses with a remark like, "Don't worry, honey; in just a few years they won't bother you at all. In fact, they won't even want you around." So I give in and talk, play, or watch *Emergency*.

Am I approachable or is my response to my children's world-view one big busy signal? What a perplexing question! Like the businessman who plugs the Muzak system into the phone line, too many fathers have succumbed to the temptation to buy off their kids with money, things, organized activities—anything to get them off the parental back.

I am reminded of this when I sit next to a mother and father at PTA who, in the more boring moments of the evening, fill out a summer camp application for their three children. They are preparing to spend six hundred dollars each week for seven weeks in order to relieve themselves of the kids for the summer. An expensive busy signal! But that is just one of the available alternatives.

In our community we have day-care centers, preschools which open at 6:30 A.M. and close at 7:00 P.M., and multimillion-dollar recreation centers which take up in the afternoon where the schools leave off. They all represent sophisticated baby-sitting arrangements so that fathers and mothers can spend their time elsewhere.

The most destructive busy signals, however, occur right in the home. Some begin with the words, *"Not now; later . . . "* Variations on that theme can be seen in the following phrases: *"Wait* until your Dad finishes the . . . " or "Can't you find *something else* to do?" or "Ask your *mother"* or "Son, Dad's awfully *tired* right now." When I researched these responses to inquiring children, it was interesting to discover that I didn't even have to leave my home. They were the words I was using; I just had to listen to myself.

I once read a wise statement by an unknown author about the problem of busy signals. He pointed out that the too busy father tends to give his children money instead of time, because he has more money than time. By this single act, he warps both their sense of practical values and family values. He said it takes a dedicated parent to cancel golf, cocktail parties, and trips to the city to spend time in ordinary talk with his young. In a pressurized world, engagements with one's own children are most easily postponable.

Pace-setting had to do with *initiating* and *motivating*, fathers talking with children. We've turned the record over now, and we are wrestling with the question of what kind of responses the effective father makes when his children talk with him. What is it that children want when they approach their fathers? What are they looking for?

Among the categories of child-oriented objectives might be these: *answers* to questions, *affection and physical tenderness, attention* to hurt or insecure feelings, and *companionship* in activity. That seems like a reasonable list of needs. Why then do we frequently find ourselves irritated, hold ourselves aloof, give busy signals when our children try to reach out and touch us?

One possibility might be that a child's needs appear to be so impulsive—so unplanned in contrast to our more ordered way of living. We've looked forward to a quiet evening in front of the fireplace, and what's more, the anticipation has sustained us all day. But the children haven't had this dream; they wish to play a game. We've been planning to spend the evening finishing off the income tax forms, but one of the kids needs help on a science project.

Perhaps another possibility is that we've been turning our backs on insignificant things all day: advertisements, meaningless conversations, hassles which did not concern us. The screening mechanism of our minds grows more efficient as the day passes, and we turn deaf ears to all but the most important matters. Our children try for just so long, and then they turn away; Dad is unapproachable today, they say. His busy signals are turned up to full volume; his words are curt; his exasperated breathing is deep; his temper is short. Stay away from Dad!

If you scan the Bible for models of the approachable father, you may be disappointed to find out how scanty the field is. In fact, the only one that really impressed me was the heavenly model.

When David, the second king of Israel, wished to discourse on the nature of his God, he often chose the expressions a son might use in reference to his father. When David wanted to express himself on themes of security, protection, stability and dependability, he found himself talking about God. God was an effective father to David. It may be an indication of how David felt about his earthly father, Jesse, who had brought eight sons into the world. It is a reasonable deduction that the boy David must have found enormous satisfaction in his father, and now as a man, he transferred those same feelings into his relationship with God.

The element of approachable fatherhood crops up in David's writings whenever he is uneasy about life. Just as a child rushes to his father when he is nervous about a situation, David found himself relaxing in the father-son relationship he had with God. Now that Jesse was an old man and David was himself an adult, his spiritual reflexes turned heavenward. He found in the vertical relationship with God that which he had discovered on a more limited basis as a child with his dad.

The issues were much larger now. David was surrounded by a hostile environment and enemies who sought his personal destruction. There were many who would have loved to see David humiliated, defeated, dethroned. No one could be fully trusted. That is a situation in which a father—an approachable father—becomes very important.

The point is this: when David called upon his Heavenly Father, there was no busy signal. And he tells us that over and over again. The Psalms are full of David's awareness that God could be reached and communicated with at a moment's notice. That was David's greatest source of comfort. His God was approachable. What qualities does David find in his approachable Heavenly Father? They may be worth studying and implementing.

Perhaps at the top of David's list of God's characteristics was the fact that his Heavenly Father had *an open and discriminating ear.* It never ceased to amaze David that God had provided an open hotline between Jerusalem and the heavenly throne. You sense David's feeling of awe about this in the eighth Psalm when he matches man against the relative expansiveness of the universe. Being a leader himself, he could reflect upon the demands that management of the universe would make. He was aware that as a king, he couldn't attend to the intricate and intimate matters of every individual subject; yet God does. In spite of the enormousness of it all, God is a listener to each of his children. "What is man," David asks, "that thou art mindful of him?"

David's view of God illustrates a child's view of his father. "Mother," a child asks, "is Daddy a good engineer?" Mother responds happily, "He's the best in the whole world; no one's better." The words she speaks are cast in affection; the words the child hears are cast in reality. The child's view of his father is based on the concept that the whole world centers on the father's activities. "My dad is important; he gets phone calls, mail, and many visitors. He has many friends, and the whole world depends upon what he thinks and does."

My children think like that. Surely, they think, I must sometime have met the President of the United States. Naturally, I must know Billy Graham. A political celebrity appears on television, and my daughter turns to me, "Do you know him, Daddy?" If I say that I do not, she reasons that the so-called personality on the news is not really that important. She measures the world by what she thinks of me.

The Heavenly Father is a busy and important "person," Psalm eight says. But God's incredible awareness of everything does not preclude his intimate sensitivity to each of his children. He has a discriminating ear open to our faintest cry. "The Lord has set apart the godly for himself; the Lord *hears* when I call" (Psalm 4:3).

That is *quality one* for the approachable father: the heavenly type of ear, never too busy to hear small things which may grow to great importance.

John Drakeford once authored a book with the insightful title, *The Awesome Power of the Listening Ear.* His title makes a great statement. The man who listens *powerfully* is effective. And that is exactly why many fathers are not effective, for in a world of endless verbiage, most men are not good listeners—at least when it comes to listening to their children.

Many fathers do not listen well because they would rather speak. They feel that what they have to say is more important than what they have to hear. There may be an ironic tragedy to that gross misunderstanding, because the man who does not know how to listen will not really know what to say.

Other fathers don't listen well because they have trained themselves to listen only to those things they feel are important. Since the interests of children are less than "important," these fathers don't listen. Children do not have information which earns more money; they don't know influential people; and they do not normally have insights or new ideas which will change our world. We'll listen to them later . . . when they grow up.

Still other fathers fail to listen because they don't know how to listen. They hear only words, little realizing that listening involves perception of many human communicative devices. For example, good listening involves the interpretation of gestures, facial expressions, word-choices, body posture, timing, context, and a host of other things.

A young father, trying very hard to be honest about his problems with his wife and children, said to me, "Frankly, I'm not a sensitive man. I am constantly discovering that my family is telling me things about themselves and their needs, and I am not hearing them. I completely miss the points they are trying to make. What am I doing wrong?"

As I talk to him and his wife, I notice immediately how far apart they are in communication. He attacks her words as a theologian might exegete a Greek phrase. But in the few minutes I am with them, I am already aware that she communicates in tones of voice, pauses, facial configurations, and gestures of hands or arms. But he is missing all of this, and thus missing her real message. I find myself sitting like an interpreter, telling a husband what his wife is saying to him. He is right; he is not sensitive. No one has ever taught him how to listen. If he cannot even understand his wife, his misunderstanding of his children must be immense.

The children of my generation were often told that "children should be seen and not heard." So, as youngsters we concluded that virtuous behavior was to sit quietly while adults talked. The implication was that nothing which came out of a child's mouth was of any significance. We could have the leftover time, when the adults were too tired or disinterested in talking further. Slack time was ours in which to express ourselves. "Be quiet, Johnny; can't you see that Grandpa is talking?"

I'm pleased that God does not believe in that unfortunate dictum. Every child, God says, is to be heard. And what's more, everything a child says will be heard; the line to Heaven is open. Perhaps after it has been heard, it will receive a rebuke, a correction, or even a retribution—but it will be heard.

Good listening takes training and discipline. Recently I was invited aboard a nuclear submarine for dinner with the commander. During a tour of the ship, I stood outside a door marked "Top secret; admission by authorized personnel only." Behind it were men and machines listening to all sorts of strange wave patterns floating across the world. Deciphered, the things which they heard could help our military people understand what the enemy was thinking and doing. These were men trained to listen—to pluck from the air significant matters and separate them from insignificant matters. That is quality one of the approachable and effective father.

Like my sailor friends, the effective father deliberately develops a facility to listen to his family—to hear what is being said, and sometimes to hear what is *not* being said. He has finely tuned his open ear to hear tones of voice, certain kinds of silence and broodishness, special styles of crying, code-words which imply frustration, heartbreak or rebellion, pained looks of distress, and slumping postures of personal defeat and discouragement. He hears the signals and interprets them.

The art of listening takes time, work, and prayer; it does not come by instinct. Conversely, it is inexcusable for any man to say that he does not have the gift of sensitivity. If he lacks it, it is because he has failed to work at it for reasons best known to himself.

The very best of us will sometimes make mistakes in this business of listening. For example, I misread my son one evening when I was preparing to take a house guest to the airport for his return home. Before we left, I turned to Mark and suggested that he go along. He immediately accepted. As we were getting our coats on, I issued the same invitation to our daughter, Kris. Out of the corner of my eye, I noticed a cloud come over Mark's face. Not reading the signals correctly, I thought I saw pure selfishness. I was sure I was right when throughout the ride to and from the airport, Mark remained absolutely silent, almost physically turning away whenever his sister spoke either to him or to me.

When we returned home, I sent Kris into the house and began to lecture him; first, for being so selfish, and secondly, for pouting when things did not go his way.

The full story came later. When I pieced things together, I found that I had missed the right signals. I discovered that his disappointment was based on the fact that he needed to discuss some things alone with me. His mind had been preoccupied with some special challenges he was facing on his soccer team and he was uneasy about them. He believed that talking with me about them might help him to meet them. I had not sensed that. Not having "heard," I gave him a kind of busy signal.

It would be hard to do an instant replay of that whole affair and find out how I could have done a better job. But it stands as an example of how a father can totally misread a child's mind. I should have seen red flags at the beginning, but I didn't. I assumed sin when I should have heard honest disappointment. Not attuned to the fact that it had been several days since he had been alone with me, I blew a chance to provide a few intimate moments. Unlike David's God, I was unavailable when my son needed me.

As a result of that experience, I learned that there are times when my children are not content to be simply part of a group, even a family group. They want and deserve prime time with Dad—alone. I listen for those times now.

When my friends on the submarine twist the dials of their sensitive receiving instruments, they know what they are listening for. But most of us fathers do not. In contrast, God does. "The Lord," David wrote, "is near to the brokenhearted and saves the crushed in spirit" (Psalm 34:18). "Even before a word is on my tongue, lo, O Lord, thou knowest it altogether" (Psalm 139:4).

Effective fathers listen for *questions*, the answers to which will shape a child's mind and spirit. It is rush hour and the traffic is snarled beyond description. A voice comes from the back seat, "Daddy, what does God look like?" Your approachability quotient hangs on how you handle that one. Is it the kind of question you've been looking for? Then traffic jams aren't going to stop you from conversation one bit. "Dad, how come the quarter-

back got thrown out of the game and he's a Christian?"
With a question like that, it is no time for a father to
throw out a busy signal even if the game is deadlocked
with only two minutes to go.

Fathers also listen for the hunger for affection and
tenderness. A child turns moody and seemingly disre-
spectful at the dinner table. A father's impulse might be
to strongly reprimand the child and perhaps even punish
him. But sensing the behavior is a bit out of character, the
father suggests that the two go to the child's bedroom for
a few minutes. "Son, your behavior at the table was unacceptable. Now if you're just testing me to see how far I'll
go, I'm ready to do something about it . . . now! But if
you're telling me that something is really bothering you
that I don't know about, I'd like you to share it with me."

The child dissolves into tears, and piece by piece the
feelings emerge. During the past few days it seems as if
every judgment call in the house has gone against him.
He feels alone. The father realizes in a moment that it
just may seem like that. He draws the boy to himself and
holds him quietly and lovingly for ten minutes while the
child sobs out his pent-up feelings of frustration and
futility. In the hugging and touching is reaffirmation.
This was not a time for punishment, and the listening
father caught the real message—just in time.

Approachable fathers are listening all the time for feelings of inadequacy. The child who constantly pesters his
parents throughout an evening may really be saying, "I
have to keep on testing you to know if you really think
I'm worthwhile and important." A daughter becomes
irritating because she keeps wanting to climb on her
father's lap and physically love him. He keeps giving her
busy signals, and she keeps persisting. But if he should
stop everything for just a few minutes and give her the
affection she seeks, he may discover that her interest

quickly subsides. She has found out what she needed to know; she's important to him.

A boy keeps downgrading himself when it comes to his ability to read. He claims he doesn't enjoy it, that he gets nothing out of it, that there are no good books, anyway. What he may really be saying is that he's not sure that he's a very good student. An hour spent with his father reading together just may turn the tide in another direction.

Approachable fathers listen for the need of companionship. "Dad, would you go up to the store with me?" "Dad, would you drive for the Cub Scouts' field trip next week?" "Dad, would you sit here for a few minutes while I go to sleep?" These are no times for busy signals.

If we know *what* to listen for, do we know *when* to listen? Again, approachability can frequently be jeopardized by a poor sense of timing. Fathers who have never learned to listen may have not caught on to the fact that one is more liable to hear valuable things at specific times of the day. Take bedtime, for example. Ineffective fathers usually miss the value of a child's bedtime because they are caught up with "significant" matters like "Monday Night Football," endless meetings outside the home, and snoozes on the couch.

But in the relaxed atmosphere of bedtime, children let down their guards and talk endlessly. To be sure, some of their willingness to talk is motivated by the desire not to be left alone or have the lights turned off. But who cares? Here it is that questions are asked, fears unmasked, and deep introspective discussions are held. Children talk about dreams, desires, regrets, and resistances.

Other special times for listening may come when children are sick, exhilarated by some sort of triumph, repentant over something done, or when a father has them to himself for long unbroken periods of time. A successful Christian father once told me that he planned at least one long trip each year with each of his children even if it meant their missing a few school days. Having now tried it myself, I understand his thinking. The special trips provide conditions not only for significant conversation, but for the planting of lifelong memories.

The more a child becomes aware of a father's willingness to listen, the more a father will begin to hear. But if a daughter comes into a living room night after night with a question only to be cut off with "Dear, wait until I finish the paper and then I'll talk with you," she will hear a more cruel translation than the surface meaning of the words. She hears, "You're not as important as the paper is; you will always be relatively unimportant."

As children grow older, we can teach them that there are times for talk and times when parents should be left alone to their own private pursuits. It's certainly reasonable that children should not have the right to intrude upon their parents at every whim. And that kind of thing can easily be taught—as soon as we have convinced our children that we are indeed approachable because we are willing to listen. Once they are assured of that, we are on our way to a more secure relationship.

A businessman I know has resigned his job and moved from a prestigious suburb. He now runs a quiet bakery business which keeps him busy, to be sure, but gives him large blocks of time to enjoy his family. I asked him why he has made such a decision.

He recalled for me a day when he and his wife and two children were driving in the car. The boy had asked his mother what the score of a certain basketball game had turned out to be.

"I suddenly realized that it was the kind of question a son usually asks his father, not his mother. I was hit with the immediate awareness that I am gone so much that the children have gotten used to addressing all their questions to their mother. She is the only one who is around all the time. She is the dependable listener. It's not that I resent my wife's knowing the score of a basketball game, but it's the shocking conclusion that my children don't think of me as an available listener. I'm either off on some trip or preoccupied when I'm home, they think. And so they develop a habit: 'Don't talk to Dad about incidentals; he's too busy to be interested.' "

That painful observation caused one man to change lifestyle. He now enjoys having time to listen to his children. He took drastic steps to guarantee to them an experience which David, king of Israel, long ago said was important to him: "I cried unto the Lord, and he heard my voice. . . . "

A second aspect of approachability—beyond the discriminating and open ear—is a quality I call *unconditional acceptance*. To put it in other words, children and teenagers are far more prone to engage in dialogue with a father who accepts them as persons, placing no conditions upon the relationship.

Long hair, prewashed jeans, loud music, and a host of other symbols of the younger generation have split more fathers from their children than can be imagined. I have met fathers who can never quite get beyond the appearance of their sons in order to have an intelligent discussion about real issues. Take the tragic admission that Sparky Anderson, manager of the World Champion Cincinnati Reds, made to reporters just before the 1975 World Series.

"It was about two years ago. I told my boy, Lee, to get his hair cut," Anderson said. "It was long and tied in a pony tail. I'd told (him) to get his hair cut before I came home again. I came home, and it wasn't cut. He was out in the garage, on his knees, fixing his motorbike. So I told him to get it cut, and he said, 'No.'

"There was no way I could win. I saw that if I wanted him to cut his hair, I was going to have to get down and whip him with my bare hands. I didn't want that. *So I just walked away. I cut him off from me. I had no communication with my boy for a year.* He talked to his mother, but not to me. I lost my boy."

What Sparky Anderson was saying is that he failed to see the difference between the person and external symbols. He placed the condition of their relationship on a relatively shallow base. What he was really saying to his son by words and action was, fit *my* values; be exactly like me, and *then* I'll accept you.

I'm sure that behind Anderson's thinking was the feeling of embarrassment. He saw long hair as a mark of rebellion. Perhaps he thought of it as being unmasculine. The long hair, therefore, became a symbol of failure as a father, or so Sparky Anderson thought.

When the baseball manager reflected upon this sad chapter in his broken fellowship with his son, he said to fathers everywhere, "Don't protect your image. That's what I was doing. There was Lee with his long hair, and there I was with my image of short hair. When we argued out in the garage, I told him, 'Someday you'll respect me as your father,' and he said, 'I already respect you.' I didn't understand how he could say that and still have long hair. I was ashamed of myself. I was being the child, and Lee was being the man. *I wasn't man enough to father my son.*"

When Isaac, the son of Abraham, grew to be a man, he fathered two sons. In a day when it was culturally permissible—but nevertheless unwise—Isaac played favorites. He was far more excited about Esau, the oldest, than he was about Jacob. There was something about Esau that turned Isaac on. Doubtless it had something to do with Esau's ability as a hunter and his strong masculine identity. He felt less attached to Jacob. Somehow Jacob didn't seem to fit his image of a hefty man. He just couldn't accept him.

Isaac's prejudice, based on external matters, affected the whole family. When Isaac neared death and it came time to pass on the inheritance of the family to the favorite son, his wife and the less appreciated Jacob entered into a plot to fool the old man. They disguised Jacob in all of the external symbols that drew Isaac to Esau: a special menu that Isaac loved, an arm dressed with sheepskin to remind Isaac of his older son's masculine physique, and all the right words. And because this was often the extent of Isaac's evaluation of his children, he was taken in.

It set in motion family struggles that would go on for years. Isaac laid a groundwork on which Jacob gained attention and advantage by deceit and deception. Long after Jacob would leave home, the dishonest streak would be his basic pattern of life. There's a very obvious moral to the story: when a man judges his children by external values and accepts them on that basis, he paves the way for relational chaos, lasting even long after his own death. Too bad that Isaac didn't find out what Sparky Anderson found out just in time.

Among the many things that fathers tend to wish from their children is emulation, respect, and agreement. It may bother us when a child begins to prefer a model of car other than the one we think is the best. Perhaps we are confused when they reject our standards of music for another. As the years pass, we make the painful discovery that their understanding of success may be different than ours. Each of these and many others set off uneasy vibrations within us. We mistake independent thought for rejection and even rebellion. Thus, if we are not careful, we begin to get irritated at our sons and daughters. Conversations tend to concentrate on surface issues, and we begin to make it plain that we are disappointed, even embarrassed over their style and evaluation of life.

Little by little we wall off large areas of conversational territory which cannot be touched. Before long, like Jacob, our children are lying to us—telling us what we want to hear only to get us off their backs. Or worse yet, they begin to tell us nothing. Communication on deep things is lost because the conditions stayed on the surface.

No book on fatherhood could ever hope to present a formula for knowing how much independence a child should have from the value systems of his parents. Perhaps the answer lies not in formulae, but rather in prayerful wisdom.

A missionary friend who fathered three handsome teenage boys, all of whom wore their hair in the long style, told me how he approached what he thought was a problem. He sat his sons down and leveled with them. "Boys, your choice of hair style turns men in my generation off. But it apparently turns the men in your generation on, and I'll accept that. If you wear your hair long because that's the prevailing style, fine. But if it is a symbol of rebellion against your father while you live in our home, then I'll wrestle each of you to the floor and cut it off myself."

The sons assured their father of their respect and love for him, and aside from good-natured kidding, the issue was never mentioned again. Perhaps that's why the sons try to get home to their parents every chance they can, now that they live in other parts of the world. They're accepted for what they are—not what they look like.

Wisdom—a gift from God—helps us discern real issues, and with it fathers become open and approachable. They accept their children on the right basis. There are no busy signals based on nonacceptance.

The effective father whose ear is open and whose wisdom makes him able to accept his children as they are, adds a final quality to his reputation for being approachable. Call it *flexible response*. To use another telephone analogy, he doesn't put his kids on "hold."

It was the middle of the night when Kris called my name. I heard her first "Daddy!" immediately and sprang out of bed and down the hall to her room. She was in distress. There had been a bad dream, and Kris was having a rough time sorting out what was real and what was part of the dream.

Why had she called her father? Because her instinct somehow told her that when equilibrium is in jeopardy, fathers can help restore balance. Her young mind had set up a pattern of response to uneasy situations: call for Dad; he knows how to make upside down things turn right side up again. So in obedience to pattern she calls, and I come.

Suppose that I choose to belittle the "dumb dream." Suppose I yell down the hall, "What do you want?" When the report comes back that she is upset over a dream, suppose I respond with, "Don't worry about it! Everything will be all right; go back to sleep."

What do I really say? Perhaps I will seem to say, "Don't dump your problems on me; work them out for yourself. Your feelings are immature and stupid; make them dissolve. But by all means, leave me alone so that I can get some sleep."

But I don't do that; I have learned that *response* to my children when they are in crucial moments is of utmost importance. I go back to David and his sense of security and read his words, "I keep the Lord before me; because he is at my right hand, I shall not be moved." Perhaps David had had some bad nocturnal moments and his father had come. Now as an adult he finds times in his life when everything seems like a bad dream. It is instinctive to cry out, and now it is not an earthly father who comes, but a Heavenly Father who is constantly effective.

All effective fathers learn the importance of a wise and flexible response to their children's calls for attention. No busy signals here. No "hold" button.

It is in our response to our children that we often set into concrete exactly what they will become. We are the most important people in the world to them for a number of years. Our opinions are the ones that count the most. Our responses to their first experimental thrusts of independent personhood will shape their personalities and world views in an almost indelible image.

Take self-expression, for example. A child dares to share a poem he has written. Gingerly he brings it to the living room where the family sits. The imagery is crude, the words misspelled, and the thought expressed is so naive that to an adult it is really quite amusing. But in sharing his thoughts, the child has actually laid his or her soul out on the carpet. Here is a crisis of response. The child is making a first tentative attempt to reach out of himself and gain affirmative reaction.

The proper response must be praise. Even if the poem is a disaster, the very act of creating it is in itself worthy of enthusiastic applause. But some fathers would dismiss the poem with laughter, and if the laughter is cutting and derisive enough, the child may not take up the pen again.

Creativity is a delicate matter, fragile at birth and nurtured by affirmation. Are we approachable when it comes to a young person expressing original and artistic ideas and capacities? We need not be insincere, praising quality where there is no quality. But in the very beginning, high marks can be given for even making the attempt.

Approachability demands flexible response, not only in creative moments, but when things go sour also. "Hear my cry, O God, listen to my prayer; from the ends of the earth I call to thee when my heart is faint" (Psalm 61:1). David's approach to God his Heavenly Father was uncowering because he knew God's responses to his struggles were fair and reasonable. Whether he had miserably failed or impressively triumphed, God was approachable.

A ten-year-old who is playing in a living room inadvertently knocks over a lamp and cracks its ceramic base. He knows that the lamp is highly treasured by his parents, and—based upon past performance—he knows that they will fly into a rage when the crack is discovered. He realizes this in an instant as he surveys the damage. As he plots his next move, he can have no thought of confession. He notices that the lamp can be turned so that the crack faces the wall and cannot easily be seen. Rather than face the issue head-on with his unapproachable parents, he elects to cover up the problem.

For weeks, however, the guilty child lives in fear of the day when someone will find the crack. Every time he sees his father or mother go near the lamp to turn it on or off, his body tenses—has the moment of truth arrived? The longer the secret is undisclosed, the more it drives a quiet wedge between him and his parents. He doesn't enjoy the living room, especially when his parents are in it. Even the objects in the room become his enemies because they are identified with the lamp whose crack is going to betray him one of these days. The anticipated response to the crack has become more significant than the original problem. But unapproachability in bad moments—"when the heart is faint"—has quenched all possibility of keeping short accounts.

Not long ago Gail and I heard the crash of breaking glass come from our living room. Running in the direction of the noise, we found our daughter behind a table where she was trying to retrieve a ball. Her foot had caught a cord, and a lamp—one both her mother and I prize—had fallen over. The globe of the lamp was in several pieces. Down deep within me was an impulse of immediate anger. I was ready to give vent to the anger because she had been playing ball in an area of the house where ball playing was out of bounds. She deserved—I thought—what my instincts prompted me to deliver.

But on the other hand, one look at her face told me that it was obvious that she knew she had been wrong. There she knelt, frozen, awaiting my response. I sensed that she was poised on the razor edge between trusting me with honest repentance or hardening into a defensive posture of excuses and passing the buck. My anger would provoke her to excuses; my understanding would give rise to her honest evaluation of her guilt.

Why is it hard to grant to children the same forgiveness we adults so desperately desire when we make mistakes? Must there be punishment for something which was done unintentionally—even if the initial act was actual disobedience? The anger dissolved, and I took her in my arms and hugged her. The tears flowed freely, and she expressed her sorrow. She now understood why we don't play ball games in the living room. But she understood something even more significant. I am approachable when she has made a bad mistake. In the future when the mistakes are even more dramatic, I want her to remember my response to the broken lamp. I want her to cry out my name instinctively, knowing that I am approachable and will respond flexibly in a mature assessment of the situation.

The approachability of fathers in the early years of

their children's lives will reduce the number of defense mechanisms their children will erect. If they experience sledge-hammer reactions in their sour moments, children will create a remarkable facility for passing responsibility, making excuses, or perhaps taking no risks at all. What father wants that? Much better that they find in their fathers—effective fathers—tender responses when their child-sized hearts are faint. Sour moments are no time for busy signals.

There is an ironic twist to the doctrine of approachability. The more approachable we are, the more we hasten the day when our children will need to approach us no longer. For as a father listens, accepts, and responds in an affirming manner, he enhances the quality of maturity. When the children "dial" their father's number, they receive no busy signal. They know that he is just a call away. It makes them take greater risks in self-development and acceptance. They grow faster and more wholesomely. And as they mature, they call less and less. They work out their own bad dreams; they develop their own ability at self-criticism in creativity. They become independent. But they do so because they know there is a man out there who never responds with a busy signal.

The unapproachable father retards growth for awhile. His children seek his attention, and due to various conflicting inputs, they do not get it. They search for correction, for affirmation, for stability, and it isn't there. They seek evaluation of their world view, but it isn't available. Children under these conditions grow slowly and often unhealthfully. Psychologically and emotionally, they remain children far into biological adulthood. Ultimately, having experienced so many busy signals, they begin to dial other numbers. There is no turning back.

Author Em Griffin has spoken poignantly of the sad results of unapproachability. In his book *The Mind Chang-*

ers (Tyndale House, 1976), he refers to a recent song, "Cat's in the Cradle,"[6] which goes like this:

> My child arrived just the other day.
> He came to the world in the usual way.
> But there were planes to catch and bills to pay.
> He learned to walk while I was away.
> And he was talkin' 'fore I knew it and as he grew
> He'd say, "I'm gonna be like you, Dad,
> You know I'm gonna be like you."
>
> And the cat's in the cradle and the silver spoon.
> Little boy blue and the man on the moon.
> "When you comin' home, Dad?"
> "I don't know when, but we'll get together then.
> You know we'll have a good time then."
>
> My son turned ten just the other day.
> He said "Thanks for the ball, Dad, come on, let's play,
> Can you teach me to throw?" I said "not today
> I got a lot to do." He said "That's O.K."
> And he walked away, but his smile never dimmed.
> And said "I'm gonna be like him, yeah
> You know I'm gonna be like him."
>
> And the cat's in the cradle and the silver spoon.
> Little boy blue and the man on the moon.
> "When you comin' home, Dad?"
> "I don't know when, but we'll get together then.
> You know we'll have a good time then."
>
> Well he came home from college just the other day

So much like a man I just had to say
"Son, I'm proud of you; can't you sit for a
   while?"
He shook his head and said with a smile
"What I'd really like, Dad, is to borrow the car
   keys.
See you later. Can I have them please?"

And the cat's in the cradle and the silver spoon.
Little boy blue and the man on the moon.
"When you comin' home, Dad?"
"I don't know when, but we'll get together then.
You know we'll have a good time then."

I've long since retired. My son's moved away.
I called him up just the other day.
I said, "I'd like to see you if you don't mind."
He said, "I'd love to, Dad, if I can find the time.
You see my new job's a hassle and the kids have
   the flu.
But it's sure nice talking to you, Dad
It's been sure nice talking to you."

And as I hung up the phone it occurred to me—
He'd grown up just like me.
My boy was just like me.

And the cat's in the cradle and the silver spoon.
Little boy blue and the man on the moon.
"When you comin' home, son?"
"I don't know when, but we'll get together then.
You know we'll have a good time then."

For David, king of Israel, approachability meant intimacy with a Heavenly Father who created the perfect
model of effectiveness.

Answer me when I call, O God of my right!
Thou hast given me room when I was in distress.
Be gracious to me and hear my prayer.
O men, how long shall my honor suffer shame?
How long will you love vain words, and seek
    after lies?
But know that the Lord has set apart the godly
    for himself;
the Lord hears when I call to him (Psalm 4:1-3).

There are no busy signals in Heaven; there are none in the home of the effective father.

THIRD PRINCIPLE

If I am an effective father . . .

it is because

I have sharpened my sensitivity to my family's needs, committed my inner being to God's laws, and fixed a foresightful eye on opportunities and hazards ahead. I want to make sure that every family experience builds my children up and matures them.

11

Life in
White Water

MARK was in the bow of our eighteen-foot canoe; I was in the stern. Tied to the thwarts between us was the duffel: tent, sleeping bags, and lots of food. The river was a boiling white—that is to say, it was running furiously, smashing around and over rocks, here and there climbing up to gunwale-high waves. We were both paddling downriver, frantically trying to keep afloat through each combination of rapids. Our "survival" depended upon being able to pick a route back and forth across the river that would avoid the ultimate disaster of tipping over and losing everything—especially our pride as great wilderness explorers.

Then it happened! A water-soaked tree lying just below the surface caught the shoekeel of our Grumman canoe and provided the split second the river needed to spin us around. In an instant we were upside down in freezing water, the canoe filled with half the river. Our equipment could be seen floating downstream.

White water is relentless and unforgiving. There is only one possible way to beat it, and that is to keep an eye 35 to 50 yards downriver, anticipating what is ahead. Entering a series of rapids is no time to begin making decisions about where the canoe should be pointed. With the practice of reasonable foresight, the paddler may manage to keep dry most of the time.

There is something about the instinct of a canoeist that reminds me of family leadership. The person in white water threading a canoe through eddies and backwashes knows something an effective father knows: you can't make effective decisions in a state of panic. There is no room for impulsive thinking. Life in the family is like life in white water: the person steering must always look ahead of the situation. No surprises allowed.

That makes me want to think about principles of foresightful family leadership. The effective father is foresightful; he is not impulsive—the very opposite. Impulsive fathers usually find themselves taken by surprise, and that forces them to act on the spur of the moment. They lose touch with the significance of circumstances about them; therefore, they overreact or underreact to many situations. Either everything seems to be a crisis or nothing is a crisis. They're never quite sure.

If you've ever been in the bow of a canoe when you weren't confident of the capacity of the person at the steering end, you know what I mean about uneasiness and insecurity. You find yourself checking to see if your wristwatch is waterproofed and your lifebelt buckled.

It's kind of frightening. But try being a member of a family where no one can fully trust the discretion of the one in charge. Same thing! Everyone keeps a kind of "lifebelt" close by.

Impulse-directed families are always on edge. Take the Bigelow family as an example. John Bigelow's home is in the full swing of crisis on a Saturday mid-morning. He had planned a family spring cleanup day, and he had made it plain that everyone was going to perform some of the chores that would spruce up the backyard, restore the garage to order, and put a few coats of paint on things like fences, drainpipes and porch floors.

It was Roger, the ten-year-old, who precipitated the storm by acknowledging his lack of enthusiasm for the whole idea. He was irritable, seemingly lazy, and he griped at every suggestion his father made about the quality and quantity of work he was doing.

Finally, John hit the roof. He called Roger several versions of an ingrate, reminding him of all that the family was always doing to make his life enjoyable. Why, his father asked, was it so hard for Roger to tie into things when he was asked to do his part? Nothing worked! The frustration peaked when Roger was banished to his room for the day. The work accomplished on cleanup day by the rest of the family was now finished in bad humor and out of sheer determination.

Where did things go wrong? Perhaps—unnoticed by John Bigelow—it began the night before when everyone was out until midnight. The family had been invited to the home of friends, and everyone had gone. Roger, in the company of other children, had stayed up long after his normal bedtime. Exhilarated by the excitement, he was alert and high when his family reached home after the twelve o'clock hour. He was full of promises for tomorrow's household activities—promises his youthful emotions and limited physical strength could not keep the next morning.

Roger's father made a strategic mistake when he expected his son to perform at top level the next day. He hadn't thought ahead—"downriver"—when he kept his boy out so late the night before. The next morning his son's reluctance took him by surprise and he showed it in his impulsive anger and unreasonable punishment. Remember, he too had been out late the night before! At no time had Roger's father used foresight. Rather, John Bigelow measured his son by adult standards, and he didn't conceal his disappointment when Roger fell short.

A foresightful father would have anticipated this morning's events on the basis of the past evening's situation. Roger's father should have reasoned that a ten-year-old simply does not have the emotional and physical reserves to respond to an extraordinary challenge on the morning after a late night out.

What were the proper choices a foresightful father could have made? He could have brought his boy home earlier on Friday night. Or he could have allowed him more time to sleep in the morning. Or he could simply have realized that the early morning behavior patterns were probably not those of an uncooperative child, but of a tired, worn-out boy. That kind of foresight the night before would have produced a different attitude and treatment. Roger and his father would not be estranged at noontime; they could have worked out the problem together.

The biblical prototype of foresightful leadership comes straight from the relationship between Jesus and his disciples. Take Peter, the enthusiastic fisherman with the quickdraw mouth. When he gave all sorts of assurances about the heroic things he was going to do in the future, Jesus responded from the perspective of anticipation and foresight. He knew Peter's capacities better than Peter did. He was aware that Peter simply could not fulfill the promises he made. While the average person would have proceeded to get tough with Peter and perhaps—in the long run—even discarded him, Jesus didn't. Why? Because he understood Peter completely. In that context of foresight, he could take Peter's promises for what they were: expressions of sincere desire and nothing else.

In the last hours before the tragic arrest in the garden, it was the foresightful Jesus who told Peter that the disciple would face some terrible moments of crisis, that instead of standing tall for the Master, he would fall flat on his face. But then Jesus tenderly capped it all off with a reminder that he would be praying for the fisherman so that, after the crisis was all over, Peter could get back on his feet and move on with the business of growing up.

The entire formula for anticipatory or foresightful leadership is found in that conversation. Jesus *knew Peter;* he *sensed the situation;* he was *ready to respond* to it; he was already *looking to the good* that would finally come out of it. Whether you choose the model of the expert canoeist in white water or the discipleship principles of Jesus, the procedure that surfaces is quite helpful to the man choosing to be an effective father. The pattern is one of *foresight:* the capacity to know one's children in terms of their situations and capabilities, the awareness of what to expect from them in each situation, and what the ultimate objective of their growing up in a family really is.

When Mark and I take our Grumman off the top of the car and slip it into the water, we're aware of the potential danger of accidents. We've tried, therefore, to learn the capabilities of our canoe—how it will perform in various situations of wind speed, depth of water, and rate of current. Beyond that, we've studied and practiced the art of canoeing; we know the rules and the consequences of breaking them. Finally, we've worked together enough so that we know how to make crucial decisions when we're out on the water.

Those three principles—knowing the stress-limits of our craft, establishing rules of conduct on the water, and creating a program for decision-making in the clutch— are all part of foresightful living on the river and in the home.

Stress-limits in the family

When we first ventured into canoeing, we were warned never to attempt challenging situations until we knew our canoe and its capacities. We learned how much weight we could shift before it would tip over. We became aware that paddling against certain wind currents was an invitation to exhaustion. We saw how much duffle could safely be carried. Since Gail swims like a rock, we had to know what the canoe could do in each situation before we took her aboard. We were sure—even if she wasn't—that we could maintain a reasonable margin of safety so that her questionable swimming talents would not be tested.

Family leadership begins with a father who knows the stress-capacities of his children. This kind of information does not come simply by comparing our children with ourselves as we were at their age. Rather, it comes from studying *them* and watching *them* in action. Each one is entirely different in responses and ideals. Being in white water with a craft whose limits of stress are unknown is disastrous. The same is true in the family, but the stakes are even higher.

When we talk about stress capacity in our children, the first and most significant area worth studying is that of the child's emotional pressures. Children travel through several stages of emotional and mental development, and the challenges of their trip "downriver" in life are as traumatic as those which any adult is facing. I see three pinnacles of emotional pressure standing out in the sequence of childhood development up through adolescence.

Call the first one *the pressure of insecurity.* It is real, and it is profound, and no one escapes it. In fact, it returns again and again until the day we die. Take a hard look at its childhood version.

Insecurity arises as the result of unsure conditions. Take those circumstances when a child is frequently left with babysitters, when a father travels for long periods of time, when there is a high level of marital conflict, if and when the family moves to another community, or if there has been sickness or death in the immediate family. These are just samples, of course, of childhood situations which result in insecurity. Adults often underestimate the capacity of small children to sense uneasy situations brewing in the home. The children may not be able to define the event or its implications, but they are well aware that something is unsteady, that status quo is in jeopardy.

Insecurity is that indescribable feeling a child has when he doesn't know what he can hang on to if something goes wrong. Watch a small child learning to ride his first two-wheeled bicycle. The one teaching him runs down the street with his hand on the back of the seat, giving encouragement and an added sense of balance. When the hand on the seat is removed, the bike rider is on his own. Everything continues as before—until the child becomes aware that the hand on the back is gone. The front wheel wobbles, and within a few feet the once-confident rider hits the ground. What happened? Insecurity! It exploded the instant the rider became aware that he was on his own.

Children need to know that there's a hand on the saddle of their lives, providing balance should anything upset their equilibrium. If they sense that the hand is missing or has become undependable, they lapse into some form of upset: a stomach ache, babyish behavior reminiscent of three years earlier, aggressiveness, and other attempts at gaining attention.

A small child feels ignored while his parents talk with friends. Everyone wonders why the youngster begins to get louder, rudely interrupting a conversation and even becoming unruly enough to break something. The impulsive father reacts with sharp reprimands which embarrass everyone. He may employ a slap or an exasperated spanking. But the behavior pattern may have emerged from a child who felt insecure, who suddenly had a need to know whether or not his father or mother really cared for him, whether or not the friends were more important than he was. A father with foresight would have sensed that this situation shouldn't be prolonged, or he would have taken pains to reassure the child at intervals so that there would have been no need for a cry for attention and affirmation.

The security need of a child is normally met by a reasonable amount of consistency in a home: consistency of schedule, stability of place, and normalcy of responsibilities and relationships. Whenever a father foresees that one of these patterns must necessarily be disrupted, he should go to extra lengths to reassure his small children about what is going to happen and how they can cope with unsettled feelings and fears.

Every few weeks I head toward the airport for a day or two of speaking or consulting in a distant place. I have noted that even an overnight trip can make children uneasy, sometimes nervous about my personal safety or simply upset because the family routine is disrupted. Knowing this, I always schedule blocks of special time just before and after a trip to compensate for this adjustment. I try to point out in conversation why I think the trip is useful, and how I think God can bring results from my travel.

If I'm successful in my reassurances, the children will not say a sad, wistful goodbye, but will join Gail in sending me off with a sense of support and anticipation for what God is planning for this time. My return is an occasion for a special time together to report the results. Now that they are older it is becoming possible to enhance this by occasionally taking one of them with me.

As our children mature, *the onset of puberty* brings a second set of emotional stresses to children to which many fathers do not sensitize themselves. If unprepared, they are unequipped to cope with the "surprises" that come in their children's pubescent behavior. Reacting impulsively to situations, they alienate their children when they should have been drawing them significantly closer.

Puberty brings enormous changes in the moods and feelings of young boys and girls. Various glands are moving into operation to trigger later adult functions. It may take several years for the new hormonal secretions to be balanced. Endocrinologists tell us that early adolescents can be overwhelmed by massive "overdoses" of one hormone or another, causing high moments of exhilaration or low moments of depression. There is a reasonable similarity between puberty and menopause: the former is the commencement of various hormonal activities, the latter the cessation of some of those same functions. Both experiences—puberty and menopause—can cause mystifying attitudes and moods which are easily misunderstood by others. Parents who do not easily understand the pubescent child should remember he is probably having just as difficult a time figuring himself out.

But the impulsive father hasn't thought this one through, because he doesn't anticipate the dynamics of puberty. So he reacts in panic and often betrays the confidence his children have in him at the very moment when they needed his reassurance the most. He demands that they explain moods that they can't control, stop crying when in fact they can't fathom why they started, and be more careful when in fact their clumsiness is an equal embarrassment to them.

Foresightful leadership would have caused an effective father to carefully study the conditions and effects of puberty long before his children arrived at that stage of life. He would then have taken great pains to share with his children what they could expect. Being a foresightful discipler of men, Jesus often helped them see the implications of what was ahead. Take the conversation Jesus had with Peter when he told him that there would soon be a time when in the pressure of the situation, Peter would appear to fall. When that time came, Peter would remember that Jesus had warned him about this situation, what was behind it, and the fact that there would be a time to pick up the pieces. Jesus' awareness of things "downriver" helped Peter pull himself together when he might have quit.

In his book *Hide or Seek*, Dr. James Dobson notes the importance of a father talking to his children about puberty. Since my older child was about to enter that period of life, I read Dobson enthusiastically. Gail and I thought that we had instructed our children carefully on the subject of the psychosexual changes that were coming, but since Dr. Dobson thought it was so significant we agreed that I would reinforce the teaching with one more conversation, just to be sure that we had passed the test.

I invited Mark to go on a walk with me, and after we had passed the conversational time of day on a number of trivial items, I said, "Have you noticed any times lately when you seem to get suddenly sad for no reason at all?" The response was immediate and assertive: "Good grief, Dad; are we going to talk about puberty again?" I guess we'd done the job. Dobson would have been proud.

Puberty has become such a fact of life about our home that it's even become a family joke. When someone responds to a problem in a less than acceptable way, another may be heard to say, "He's just going through puberty." Not only does it remind us all that there is such an experience, but it does lighten the moment. Perhaps it went a bit too far when one morning everyone sensed irritability in me. When Gail asked, "What's wrong with you this morning, dear?" Kristen answered for me rather quickly: "Don't worry, Mom; Dad's just going through puberty today."

Beyond the period of puberty, a father has to anticipate the emotional stress created by adolescent *competition* and *pride*. These twin struggles appear to face almost every teenager as he or she tries to find a role in society. The extremes are found in the *overachiever* who always has to win and the *underachiever* who becomes apathetic and indifferent to what happens. These symptoms can be equally dangerous. If a father is foresightful, he can spot the roots of these patterns long before they become set in concrete behavior. The competitive instinct will appear in the way children play games. Do they have to win every time? Do they go to pieces when their side loses?

I watched a Little League catcher slowly go to pieces during the middle innings of a ball game as his club gave up a series of runs to its closest challenger for the championship. A couple of errors by an outfielder and a second baseman brought him close to uncontrolled rage. When the umpire called a baserunner safe at third because he slid under the tag of the infielder, the boy dissolved into tears. I watched him come to bat and swing for the fences and miss three times. He flung the bat back to the bench, slammed the safety helmet to the ground, and then tried to claim that the pitcher was throwing illegal pitches.

What intensified my interest in this situation was the fact that the boy's father was the team's coach. The winning instinct had been passed from father to son, and the fruit of that compulsion was in full bloom as the game progressed. Being a student of people, I gradually lost interest in the game and concentrated my attention upon the Little League catcher and his father-coach. Rather than rebuking the boy for his unrestrained conduct, the father literally egged him on by his own anger and frustration. When in the later innings their team managed a rally to come from behind and win, I watched father-coach and son-catcher run and grab each other in a frenzy of excitement. They had achieved the only thing they thought worth having: another victory. I think I watched a boy headed for trouble that day, basically because he didn't have a father foresightful enough to see in a nine-year-old boy some patterns of behavior that would betray him some day when people disagreed with him, when he would fail in a business venture, or when he would come head on with someone who was simply more skilled in some area than he was.

Foresightful fathers are sensitive to the fact that their teenaged offspring are fiercely pride-oriented. Girls will worry about their appearance; boys about their size. In the drive to assert their identity and integrity, they will find it very hard to admit that they are misinformed, that they are ignorant of something, or that they made a mistake. In the mind of the adolescent, failure is a final disaster that is larger than life.

A daughter is ignored by a boy in whom she has invested many hours of fantasy and flirtation. A son has dreamed of a starting position on an athletic team; now he has been bested by a competitor. For a girl headed for such a fall, a foresightful father prepares to help her through the inevitable despair and plans how he can reassure her that she will probably not end up being a spinster due to this defeat. Knowing that his son may or may not succeed athletically, he contemplates his role of either deflating destructive pride or inflating a destroyed spirit. His preparation for these roles must begin ahead of time; he must keep an eye "downriver." The father who is not prepared to face these things with his children will find himself dealing with situations on treacherous impulse, not on the solid ground of preparedness.

The children of the effective father face not only emotional stresses, but the tyranny of adolescent *peer pressure*. I observe that it begins to touch a human being significantly somewhere about the sixth grade level, at an age of eleven or twelve years.

Peer consciousness appears to commence at the moment that boys and girls first evidence an interest in the opposite sex. My son Mark permits me to quote him on the subject when I remind him that his one aim in life used to be to remain unmarried so that he could be a dolphin trainer and enjoy a monkey, a boa constrictor, and a German Shepherd for pets. Since he thinks girls are generally uninterested in such things, Mark always made it plain that he had no place for girls in his life.

The change of values came in *one seven-day period*. As if a curtain had been drawn shut on one lifestyle and opened dramatically on another, monkeys, boa constrictors, and German Shepherds were traded for interest in A Girl. Along with this came a new kind of friendship with boys. No longer were conversations restricted to discussions about soccer and baseball. They took on a new and vast dimension: which boy liked what girl, and which girl liked what boy.

I began to overhear long conferences on the phone about who had said what about whom. It became important to dress in a special way and to make an appearance at certain functions. The opinions of the group prevailed —binding on each individual. It became essential to master a special vocabulary and know its proper use at the appropriate moment. I think I heard a growing tendency toward a subtle but ruthless segregation: the "in's" feeling rather self-righteous as they compared themselves favorably to the "out's."

As a father I was informed of things I must do and not do, lest I embarrass my children in front of their peers. I might have been tempted to disregard this if I had not fortunately remembered that I had had the exact same fears, at the same age, in the same situations. I could either become impulsively frustrated by my son's new peer-oriented behavior and alienate him by abusing the system, or I could use foresight and help him see it through with reasonable restraint and well thought out counsel.

When we examine the dynamics of peer pressure, foresight becomes absolutely essential if father and teenager are going to maintain solid relationships. Take, for example, the clash which occurs when a fourteen-year-old girl accepts a date from a boy in her church youth group without consulting her parents. Her father and mother have repeatedly informed her that she would have to be fifteen before she could date. But she thought the rule was hazy in terms of its definition of a date. Is a date an event where two people of the opposite sex go out for an evening together? Obviously! But is it a date if six people go to a function and the group of six just happens to be made up of three boys and three girls, all having a special attraction to each other? Is that a date? That's what her father has to decide when he finds out about the plans.

If he turns his thumbs down on the proposition, he humiliates his daughter, who has to inform her "date" and the group that she must back out. A foresightful father tries as hard as he can to maintain communications and definitions with his teenaged sons and daughters so he will not be forced into making these kinds of decisions which are tinged with the pressure of peers—decisions which are made too late.

These three emotional struggles—insecurity, puberty, and peer-orientation—are just samples of the kinds of struggles for which a foresightful father must prepare himself as the years pass. But the list does not stop there.

Foresightful leadership requires a certain sensitivity to *youthful fatigue.* We're back to young Roger Bigelow who needed a father who understood that life simply does not go on as consistently for a youngster with a tired body and mind as it does for an adult. Peak adult strength brings us a large capacity for physical and mental energy. We can go on at a hectic pace for long periods of time before we begin to show the results of fatigue. But at least three kinds of people cannot do this: old people, sick people, and children.

We discovered something about the effects of fatigue in our youngest when she went off to school. In conference, her kindergarten teacher mentioned troublesome patterns of irritability, restlessness, and "whiney-ness." She asked about Kristi's bedtimes.

We said that although we tried to have Kristi in bed by 7:30 every evening, it was hard to meet that deadline every night. So, we acknowledged, bedtime tended to fluctuate.

Kristi's teacher was quite blunt with us, and we were thankful that she was. She strongly advised us that our daughter needed a consistent bedtime virtually every night of the week. There might be an occasional exception, but we could not permit an uneven schedule and expect a six-year-old to be alert and to perform well each morning. It was painful to follow that advice. Gail had to drop out of some evening activities that I enjoyed having her attend. Sometimes I had to arrange to be at home so that Gail could meet her obligations. But Kris's bedtime became an important priority. Within days there was a noticeable difference in her school work and behavior.

The frightening thing is this. We could have pinned the guilt for her behavior patterns solely on her. It is conceivable that we could have fretted, and scolded, and punished over a behavior that was really our fault. How often does that happen?

How many times do impulsive fathers punish their children for behavior that is the result of fatigue? The reality is that we are more prone to sin—child or adult—if we are physically exhausted.

A young boy plans a heavy weekend with his friends. Friday night he goes skating with the gang and comes home at 10:30 P.M. He is up early Saturday morning to rejoin the boys, and they play together all day. That evening there is a birthday party, and again he comes home exhilarated by the fun, but obviously exhausted. The next morning he is at church for both Church School and worship service. At lunchtime he receives a phone call from the fellows suggesting that they should spend the afternoon skating again. When he asks if he can go, his father says, "No."

"Why, Dad? There's nothing to do around here. Look, the guys will laugh at me if I tell them I can't go." His eyes grow red and his voice takes on a desperate tone. The impulsive father is tempted to give in to this on-slaught of "reasonable" arguments. It is easier to give in than face the consequences of an angry son. The impulsive father finally says, "All right; I guess so."

The foresightful father weighs the amount of time spent in recreation over the weekend, the fatigue involved, and the heavy school day ahead. He says, "No," and he must mean no. He will not change his mind. He carefully explains to his son—who is in no mood to listen —that it is not necessary to have a big reason or program for which to stay home. There simply needs to be time for relaxation and relative quiet.

The boy doesn't understand at all. Why? First, because he is impulsive himself—not foresightful. But second, he doesn't understand because he is just too tired. When Monday morning rolls around, the fathers of the other boys will wonder why they have to yell angrily to get their kids out of bed for school. Why they have to strong-arm their sons to stop them from teasing their sisters. Why breakfast is a relational disaster. They fail to see that it has something to do with the fact that they didn't give foresightful leadership the day before and call a good thing to a halt before it became a bad thing.

Take a look at a third category of need. Foresightful leadership requires a sensitivity to struggles within the human spirit of a young person. As adults, we allow ourselves a considerable amount of flexibility for our inner conflicts. We can pass off our sharp words with a quick "I'm not myself today." We expect forgiveness for our mistakes, understanding for our failures. It is easy, however, to be less charitable to children.

An *impulsive* father is liable to treat every action of his children with the same response. He has not taken the time to look into the circumstances and ask *why* the behavior is as it is. He does not allow his children the "reasonable" flexibility of having bad days when nothing appears to be going right. He has not sensed that there are moments when a child wonders if he is of any value as a human being, whether or not he can ever amount to anything, whether or not he can ever please anyone, whether or not God made a mistake in creating him.

As a child grows, he will begin to face the question of the ground of his own spiritual convictions: who is God and what claim does he have upon one's life? We may hope that a child will follow in the faith of his father, but that is quite different from just living in the pattern of his father's faith. Thus, the inner conflicts grow as he grapples with questions like, what does it mean to pray? And why should one pray? And what difference does God really make? And are the things that God apparently expects of one really the best things?

The foresightful father expects these struggles and prepares himself for the days when his offspring will pass through them. He is ready with the answers to questions when they're asked because he has meditated, studied, and prayed. But he also learns the subtle difference between force-feeding and gently offering spiritual food based on a mature perspective.

By contrast, the impulsive father flies off the handle every time he senses that his children are departing from the accepted way or conviction. He blames the school for its "atheistic" teaching, bans certain friendships because of their untoward influence, and unthinkingly condemns all kinds of input from the "world" because of the evil power of secular persuasion.

What he does, however, in addition to alienating his son or daughter, is begin to focus suspicion upon his ability to think things through objectively. At the very time he should have been raising his credibility as a sound and practical thinker, he is lowering it and demonstrating why it might not be wise to tell Dad everything one is thinking. Dad simply doesn't "understand."

A boy in his junior year of high school drops by to see me at my home. It takes a while to uncover the real purpose of his surprise visit, but when the story comes out, it is fraught with sadness. He has been seeing a girl whose faith is very different from the spiritual tradition in which he has been trained. In terms of daily activities and interests, the boy and his girl have much in common. But they don't go to the same kind of church, and her parents' lifestyle is distinctly different from that of the parents of the boy in my living room.

He says he loves her. Their relationship is quite important to him because he finds in her a wealth of companionship and understanding that he has never experienced before. As an advisor I sense that I have been brought into something which is complex and potentially volatile from a number of viewpoints. I am very careful to point out to him the fact that it is indeed dangerous to permit one's feelings to grow intensely loyal to a person who does not share the same experience of faith in God. From my adult perspective, it seems obvious that two people cannot ultimately share a lifetime of human experience if the ground of their faith and life is different. One of two things will finally suffer: their faith and loyalty to God or their confidence and commitment to one another.

I say it, and at the same time I know that he does not understand it. How can he perceive the dynamics of human relationship which take place in the marital context? For him, the whole matter seems to center on the problem of legality and obedience. Will he "buy" his folk's viewpoint? Will he give up a tender experience for the harsh realities of a religious structure which is often not very real to him?

He thinks he loves her and that conviction clouds all other long-range considerations. I think, on the other hand, by principles based on hindsight and foresight. They come from years of growing in my beliefs, many observations of others, and my personal experience of a marriage set in a mutual relationship to God. To me it is all so obvious; he walks on dangerous ground.

But equally detrimental is the attitude of his parents. So terrified are they that their son will "get serious" with a non-Christian girl, they are prepared to go to any lengths to break up the relationship. They assume that a sixteen-year-old boy can turn off his feelings of affection with the flick of an emotional toggle switch. They think that in response to their persuasion, threats, or warnings he can control his entire inner force of loving. Ground him; deny him privileges, they think. Thus they seek to help him find what they say is "best for him." But while they act from a kind of parental love, they act impulsively. Not understanding him, they alienate him from themselves. Their concern and conviction do not attract him.

Naturally, I share their alarm. But when I talk with them I try to persuade them that they only intensify the conditions which sent their son in the direction of his girlfriend in the first place. The opinion of the parents is based on mature convictions which have taken years to develop. The boy, on the other hand, is in a transition period: moving from his father's faith to his own—the "faith of his fathers." But that faith may not be stronger than his emotions . . . yet. His parents do not see this; in fact, they refuse to see it. They fear that admitting that his faith is not strong would be an admission of their own failure.

It is a war between their convictions and his emotion,

and they must quickly realize that they run the risk of winning the battle by force but losing the war through insensitivity. They may batter his resistance down by sheer parental power, but in so doing they may sow seeds of resentment between him and themselves. He will equate their lack of respect for his love with a callousness on the part of God.

What they must face is that he has found in his teen-age romance a type of companionship he had not discovered at home or with young women he knew to be in the way of his faith. At this point another person has emerged who fulfills at least that part of his conscious needs which are more on the surface of awareness than anything else. His parents must cope with this. The use of force may only sharpen or enhance his determination to move further away from them and (therefore) God.

A foresightful father could prevent a family crisis like this. Long before the time when a son enters the dating period of life, a foresightful father would talk with his boy about the problems which emerge in relationships where faith is important to at least one of the two people involved. It would not be adequate simply to keep preaching about the fact that Christians should not date non-Christians. Without ever coming to that point, a foresightful father could spend time developing spiritual priorities which make the decision an obvious one. It is of no help to say that one should not date non-Christians, especially when a young person spies a boy or girl who is extremely attractive, appealing, and accessible. Laws do not help then—only a carefully developed value system cultivated years in advance.

But having neglected that, a father must do the next best thing. He cannot successfully fight this relationship which my friend in the living room describes. Rather, he must seek to reaffirm the son—perhaps even trying to make up for the lack of relationship which caused the boy to be attracted to his girl in the first place. He will be wise if he encourages the boy to bring the girl home to meet the family, to enter to some extent into the family experiences where she can see the kind of life the family lives. Perhaps she will benefit from it and discover something about God that she did not know. There are a number of possible results.

The first possibility is that the girl—seeing a walk with God which is real and vital—might be led to make a similar commitment. Another is that she would see a general lifestyle which surrounds the young man and decide that this is not what she wants. A third is that the boy will be so profoundly affected by his parents' affection and acceptance that he will be drawn back to the values which cause them to be that way. Any of these possibilities is vastly superior to the state of things as I find them with the young man who comes to see me in such desperation.

But let us move on to another matter of leadership. A foresightful father is always aware of patterns and trends of opinion and influence he sees in his children. He listens to their informal conversation and evaluates their view of things. He watches their performance in critical situations and looks to see if their responses are positive and healthy.

A father monitoring a casual conversation at the dinner table picks up signals that a child has disrespect for a teacher at school. He suddenly realizes that this is the third time in ten days that he has heard something similar. *This* is the time to do something. Are these remarks a result of substandard performance or unfairness of a professional educator towards students? Or is he hearing the first subconscious attempts of a child to explain why his grades are poor? *Now* is the time to find out what is going on. The impulsive father may wait and reap the consequences at report card time. Many weeks will have passed during which a child's attitude toward his school experience could sour and set the stage for many years of academic problems.

A sudden resistance to Church School attendance in the fifth grade girls' class ought to be the signal for seeking out an explanation. Has a daughter had a bad experience with friends? Is the teacher doing a poor job? What is the root cause of a lapse in faithfulness for the disciplines of the Christian life? The foresightful father spots trends and explores meanings. An impulsive one may jump explosively into the matter long after it is too late to rescue a downhill situation.

Foresightful fathers quietly observe the behavior of their children after they have spent a day or a weekend with certain friends. They watch to see if their children are being influential or influenced, and if the latter, in what direction. A man listens to his children evaluate people and events. Is there a strain of negativism, a critical attitude, or a feeling of superiority?

He notes descriptions of events and watches to see that his children are able to evaluate themselves and their situations honestly and accurately. The ultimate acts of deception and dishonesty begin with small exaggerations and rationalizations left untouched by a father who is not looking at things from the long view, foresightfully.

Finally, a foresightful father is watching for conflicts that arise among family members. When our children were smaller, for example, we discovered that a conflict would be sure to start during a long automobile trip. As the captain of the family ship, I had two choices: I could seek to defuse conflict before it developed or deal with it in anger and frustration after it exploded. The latter was upsetting and it always destroyed the enjoyment of the trip for everyone. The former course insured sanity.

I discovered that we could expect conflict between the children when there were differing opinions about what TV shows to watch. As the children grew a few years older and began to have friends visit our home, we saw that conflict easily arises when one child has visitors and the other doesn't. When we have purchased something significant for one child and nothing for the other we can expect that jealousy will spark conflict. The child who received nothing may feel pressed to test the family situation to make sure that the balance of love is still in force. To whose side will the parents spring? Conflicts arise for the same reason when one child has done something which receives high recognition, such as an award at school, playing on an athletic team, being praised for some special thing done around the house.

If one watches for patterns of behavioral clash, he can be prepared for conflict and can learn how to prevent painful moments which the family ought not to experience. Not all conflict is either unhealthy or unspiritual, of course. Not all conflict is unavoidable, and fathers and mothers cannot feel guilty or inadequate when the best behaved of their children becomes defensive or argumentative. It happens; they are human. But when we become aware that certain types of clashes are happening with growing frequency and that they become destructive to the unity of the family, then it is time to find ways to avoid the conditions in which such problems emerge.

So what do you do with automobile trips in which there is great excitement at the point of departure and civil war at the time of arrival? In our case, Gail and I learned to have a family conference before the trip began. We reminded the kids that shouting, wrestling, and various sudden noises were not only distracting to the driver (usually me), but they were painful to everyone's ears (especially mine) in a confined place like an automobile. We recognized that fighting over seemingly meaningless issues in a car often happens, but that our car was going to be an unusual exception: conflict and uproarious behavior would not be permitted. I informed the kids about the consequences of unsettled behavior and what I was prepared to do about it.

Further, we supervised the choice of toys and books for the trip which would adequately occupy time. We found ways for the children to be helpful, such as studying the map, looking for road signs, and making a thorough search for all fifty U.S. license plates. When ground rules have been so established, and enough diversions provided, violence in the car has usually been reduced to a tolerable minimum. And so it is in the home and in any other situation where one sees a pattern of potential trouble. Stop it before it starts.

An exhaustive review of all the points of potential stress in the first eighteen years of a son or daughter would fill volumes. I have chosen a few outstanding examples in the hope that they would provoke an awareness of how we must act as effective and foresightful fathers. The name of the game is anticipation, being sensitive to the places where there are going to be problems so that we can move confidently with a plan of responsible action.

But just knowing the stress points is not enough. Preparing ourselves for a response is the next step. That's what we found in the canoe, and that's what I've found as a father.

Laws and convictions in family living

Canoeing in white water taught me a second principle of foresightful leadership in the family. Not only was it

important to learn the limits of operation of our eigh-
teen-footer, but it was imperative that we acquaint ourselves with certain rules of behavior when on the water.

Can a canoe turn over in the middle of a quiet, lazy
river just three feet deep? Absolutely!—if someone decides to stand up and wave violently to a friend on the
shore. We found that out fast! Rule number one, we
learned the wet way, is that one *never* stands in a canoe,
waves violently, or shifts weight in a sudden manner.
There were a few lessons we learned the hard way, and
it soon became obvious that we had to sit down as a
family and determine the laws of behavior for water
safety.

That's very much like what has to happen in a family
as it grows up together. Families need rules for living
together—rules which are probably few in number but
inviolable in observance. The man who does not believe
that and allows his family to exist in an atmosphere of
constant uncertainty will reap the result: an unstable
home life in which relationships are undefined and probably exploited. He will find himself trying to demand
good behavior on the strength of his own forcefulness,
and he'll have to make up impromptu rules as he goes
along. Any way you look at it, his home will be a step
short of disaster all the time.

When I analyze our own family rules, I discover that
they fall into two categories: *laws* and *convictions*. Laws
are those matters of behavior which are not open to interpretation. We did not dream them up. They were given
to us from the Scriptures by God himself. Laws are the
unnegotiable, profound forms of behavior which every
human being has to learn or face serious consequences.
The ten laws of God given to Israel on Mount Sinai are
good enough for any family, and they form the base for
behavior in our home.

Convictions, on the other hand, are those standards of conduct which the family decides to maintain because they believe them to be right for them. Certain convictions or standards may differ from person to person, family to family. We should not judge another person or family because they do not share our convictions, nor should we count ourselves as superior to or more spiritual than another whose convictions are different. The important thing is, however, that we form and submit ourselves to certain convictions which we believe to be right and healthy for our style of life.

Let's talk about laws—at least a few of them. Take a regard for truthfulness, for example. Respect for truth is something that should be established at the very beginning of childhood. It was an issue that God said was important when he first confronted Israel with his plan of righteous living.

My youth was marked by the emphasis which my father placed upon telling the truth—whatever the consequences. In my earliest childhood, he made it plain that lying would be met with the severest of punishments. Truthfulness, on the other hand, would be enthusiastically affirmed. I soon found out that he meant what he said. It was better, I learned, to own up to bad behavior than to attempt to cover it up—Watergate style. He had a way of finding things out, and improper behavior compounded by lying was the ultimate in family crime at our house. If such an occasion arose, he threw the book at me. I'm glad he did.

My father did see this thing both ways, and he was equally diligent about accepting, affirming, and rewarding me when he knew that I had faced the truth, even when it was painful.

By the age of five or six, truth telling had become an automatic thing. I remember the day when the observance of this basic rule of family conduct really paid off. Someone had set the underbrush on fire in an empty lot near our home. Before long the firemen arrived with their hoses and went to work. Right behind them were the police with their questions. Someone pointed the finger of suspicion at me since it was apparently known that I had been seen that day with matches in my hands. It didn't take long for the policeman to become quite sure I was guilty.

I remember my father taking me aside and saying, "I'm just going to ask the question once: did you have anything to do with the start of the fire?" My negative answer was all that he needed. He never asked a follow-up question. He never demanded any kind of proof. He never had to. My word was sufficient. He informed the police that I was not guilty, and they resumed their investigation. Later in the day, another boy confessed to the arson, and I learned the inestimable value of establishing my credibility.

I would like to suggest that my father was a foresightful man. He had known that there would come times when truth telling would be absolutely essential. In order to avoid impulsive reaction when a crisis arose, he had ground into me a regard for truth and the habit of facing it, no matter what the result. When the moment came in which truth was all-important, he could trust my word. That was my Dad's day when foresight paid off. Mine too!

There are other basic laws for family relationships, and one of them is *respect for those in authority*—essentially one's elders and those who fill special offices in our society. There are people to whom all of us must submit: teachers, policemen, spiritual leaders, etc.

Don't confuse *respect* for authority with inability to disagree; there's a difference. What we are talking about is the early childhood teaching that there is no place in the home for sarcasm, ridicule, unrestrained anger, or questioning the right of those in authority over us to make judgments which will prevail.

The foresightful father will establish this principle early in the life of the family. He must emphasize the children's total respect for their mother, for example. He makes it plain that behavior which undermines the role of those in authority is unthinkable and will not be tolerated. If he means what he says, disrespect simply will not happen.

Obedience is a third law which springs from the first two. A father sets obedience as a high priority in his children's lives because he knows there are potential moments when automatic obedience may be the thing which saves a life. In the earliest years, a child should be taught to obey his parents as a reflex. The Bible makes that very plain. Obedience should never be tied to the question "why?" As a child grows older, a parent will explain his decisions more and more. But first a child must learn to obey, not because there is a reason but because it is his parents' wish.

Some parents reject this notion. To require blind obedience, they suggest, is to hinder a person's ability to make good decisions on his own. But obedience is based on the concept that the one in authority is issuing his commands for the child's good. If we are never taught to obey our parents, we will never learn how to obey God. The two go hand in hand.

If obedience has been given a high priority in the earliest years, it will become less and less necessary for a parent to restrict his children through sheer command in the later years. They will have been given a basic order of life upon which they can build independently as they mature.

There are other basic laws of family life which are inviolable, but these three seem especially significant. I suggest that if basic laws—and there are not too many— are established, the foresightful father will have defused about 85 percent of the classic family explosions that arise when there are no convictions or laws.

It needs to be added here—and it will be enlarged upon later—that the only thing worse than not having laws in a family is laying down laws *but not enforcing them.* This makes children uneasy and unable to discern what is right and wrong. It develops conditions in which disregard for other laws will grow in later years.

On the foundation of laws in family life the foresightful father should build a second level of control: a series of understood *convictions* which are based on his understanding of the Scriptures. With his wife, the foresightful father establishes patterns of behavior in which the two believe and to which the family will subscribe. When crises come, there will be no need for panic, if family leaders can act out of understood and well-developed convictions.

Convictions are those matters we judge to be right or wrong, healthy or unhealthy for us. They are the hands and feet of our commitment to God. They are there when we must make decisions. If there are no convictions on central matters of life, then fathers and mothers must blurt out decisions under pressure. Not prepared, their thinking is likely to be shallow, their decision ill-considered.

A boxer trains for hours, developing his reflexes so that he can ward off his opponent's blows. He disciplines himself to develop various combinations of punches which will emerge from sheer instinct at the right moment. He knows that, once in the ring, he cannot think about every move. There is no room for panic after the match has begun. The reflexes must be so finely tuned and trained that action comes automatically.

The man of God who wishes to be an effective father trains himself. He listens to the voice of God's Spirit as it comes through the Scriptures, through the teaching and counsel of spiritual leaders, and he meditates in his own inner being upon God's best. He develops series of convictions or beliefs which he will not compromise. Call them spiritual reflexes because they give him a firm base from which to make instant decisions and evaluations. As his children grow and learn his convictions, they find security in a consistent order of things. If the convictions are sound—well thought out and reasonable —his children will respect him and perhaps adopt them as their own.

Among the convictions which our family has is that of loyalty to God and to the people of God. Our children would not ask to do something on Sunday morning which conflicts with the worship of the Lord because they know it is a family conviction that everything else is secondary to this commitment to the church family.

We have a conviction about family loyalty—that God has brought us together and that we owe a certain faithfulness to each other no matter what the situation. We may disagree energetically with one another over issues when we are in our home, but when one of us is in trouble, we stick together. Our children have found this out in a multitude of ways. When they have faced an emergency at school where they need something, they know their mother and father will do their very best to come to their aid.

Recently, our oldest was preparing a school project which made it necessary for him to get up extremely early every morning for a week. It was an opportunity to share a joint hardship and he was impressed that I would arrange to get up with him and keep him company as he worked through the dark hours of a winter morning. An act of this sort establishes a conviction: that we stick together and uphold one another.

We have a conviction that our family will join together and spring to the aid of people we know are in trouble. God has blessed us in many ways, and we feel compelled to share those blessings. We have set ourselves to serving other people as a family. When guests come into our home, each of us takes on the added tasks which extend hospitality. The ultimate benefit and blessing from giving is equally distributed among us all.

We have convictions about dating ages, dating circumstances, and times for arrival home. Gail and I have carefully explained ground rules for the kids long before individual decisions have to be made. This prevents us from being arbitrary at the last minute and conveying the feeling that we are simply trying to interfere with the children's "fun."

As a father who believes in the principle of foresight, I have tried to establish an order of personal living that will help our children see the importance of healthy living. My wife and I have a conviction about the use of alcohol and tobacco, overeating, and the misuse of money. There are many things we could have purchased both for ourselves and for the children, but we have painfully developed the ability to say a reasonable number of "no's." While we may be able to handle some of these things responsibly, we are not sure that our young children can do so. It is better to practice some restraint than to splurge—and discover when it is too late that you have launched children into the world who can't control their materialistic desires. With such convictions, the foresightful father looks "downriver" and he sees what must be done now to prepare for the future.

NASA—the space flight people—call it contingency thinking, and I think they taught us something about problem solving. When they set out to put a man on the moon, one of the key parts of their program was to anticipate every possible thing that could go wrong. Vast volumes were put together, detailing every potential problem and the proper response. They simply refused to be surprised. Those of us who followed the manned space flight program can remember a number of occasions when things went wrong that could have taken the lives of astronauts. But on almost every occasion, problems were solved immediately because the scientists had prepared themselves in advance.

A foresightful father does that. Talking with other fathers, he develops a vast catalogue of experiences and proper responses. He studies the Scriptures, reaches into his own experience, and formulates key reactions to circumstances which could arise in his home.

Knowing that one of his kids is liable to ask to go out tonight on the spur of the moment, what will his answer be? Sensing that a boy has been ignoring his school work, how can he plan an occasion on which they can talk it through? Aware that his daughter has been spending a day with some other girls who are known to have poor relationships with their parents, how will he react if she comes home and tests her parents' authority? What are the contingencies? A foresightful father is always thinking one further step "downriver." He knows the laws and convictions which bind his family and he is prepared to enforce them.

Decisions that keep you dry

Speaking of canoeing brings to my memory a rather funny incident which happened on the White River in

Vermont. I had invited a couple of friends who were unacquainted with the art of steering a canoe through white water. My first mistake was to put them both in the same craft. They were overturned and soaked within three minutes.

I should have known better than to let them go it alone, but they seemed confident. I watched them trying to choose the best way to paddle the river. It seemed that when the bowman wanted to paddle right, the sternman pushed left. Instead of keeping their canoe straight in line with the current, their indecision inevitably caused them to drift sideways. In such circumstances it's just a matter of minutes if the river is in a vengeful mood. It was, and they were in the water the first time they went over a ledge sideways.

When an effective father looks downriver in the life of his family he has to be prepared to make good decisions. And good decisions rely on a sound decision-making process. My friends in the overturned canoe had not taken time to determine who was in charge and how they would communicate with each other when a decision had to be made. It cost them a drenching. In a family, the same problem may cause lifelong disaster.

I think the foresightful father has to prepare himself for some painful leadership decisions upon which will hang his future relationship with his children. That's why it's wise to have the process of decision-making well in hand and practiced before the moment of truth. When I think of downriver decision-making, I think of a number of principles that I am using every day in dealing with my children. My job is to keep us all "dry."

If I am to be a foresightful father, the first thing I have to consider is the personal history and present condition of the particular child with whom I am involved. Since every child is different, each decision is going to be unique. I must never allow myself to fall into the trap of premature decisions or conclusions based on inadequate data. This is an important principle when the child asks permission for an event, deserves punishment for an offense, or presents a problem for solution.

I watched a man use this principle one year at a family camp. While we were visiting together, his wife came to tell him that she strongly suspected that their six-year-old had taken fifty cents out of her billfold. When she had thought back through the morning's activities, it dawned on her that he had carefully plotted the crime, telling her to wait for him on the path while he returned to their room for something he needed. He apparently used that moment to empty his mother's wallet. When confronted, he had denied any knowledge of the missing coins. Now it appeared that stealing was compounded by lying.

The impulsive father would have probably found the child and badgered him into a confession. The punishment would have been harsh, and the matter ended as a sick memory for all involved. I watched my friend think the matter through before he did anything. The three of us talked for several minutes, trying to discern the reason why a child who had never stolen before would do so on this occasion.

Stealing is a sin, but it is often important to know *why* the sin occurred. Were there conditions that *prompted* it? Were there conditions that could have *prevented* it? If we as Christians sincerely believe that we could all fall into almost any kind of sin if we did not keep ourselves from exposure to temptation, then we must also ask about the tempting conditions when we deal with the sins of our children.

My friend did just that. He learned from our conversation that most of the children in the family camp, with the exception of his son, had received allowances from their parents to spend at the camp store. The boy had been deeply hurt as he saw his camp friends purchase candy and other items at the store while he was unable to do so. When he had asked for money, his parents had refused, supposing that it was unnecessary. Thus they had created a condition in which stealing became an overwhelming temptation. The sin was his, but the context of the sin was shared.

The boy's father took that into account when he confronted him with what he knew. He shared with his son that he had become aware that other children had money and were spending it, that he had made a mistake in not allowing his son to have some spending money, and that he could see why one might be tempted to take a few coins from mother's wallet. Could this have been the case? When the child saw that his father understood the situation even more clearly than he did, he confessed that he had indeed stolen the fifty cents.

Punishment was severe, but the conversation which surrounded the situation was salted with the admission that the parents had also made a mistake. The father settled on an allowance after the sin had been confessed and paid for, and life was resumed in an atmosphere of forgiveness and restoration.

We must know the context of the matter and the background of the person involved if we are going to make good decisions on the affairs of our children. As an individual, each child must be evaluated on the basis of his particular needs and weaknesses. A foresightful father does not make a decision until he knows all of this.

A second criterion for foresightful decision-making involves the future tense. What is the *long-term growth* dimension of the decision? The foresightful father is not a baby-sitter; he is part of the process in which a human being is being sculptured. The chiseling process may at times be painful; it may appear at times to be quite out of perspective. But the sculptor knows what he is creating; therefore, he is patient and deliberate. His work is based on the future.

I have found it necessary to have repeated conversations with my children in which I have reminded them that certain decisions do not appear to them to be reasonable. I don't expect them to see the logic of everything that I ask of them. That is because they think only of the present. But I try to think of the future and where the particular matter is going to take them.

As a prep school student, I had the privilege of running track and cross-country for Mr. Marvin Goldberg of the Stony Brook School. As a Christian, Goldberg believed that all athletics were aimed at the development of character and integrity in the human experience. Year after year, he turned out championship teams and individuals. But more important, he turned out men whose adult lives were marked by many of the experiences he created for them on the track.

I remember my own personal decision to quit the cross country team in my senior year so I could—as I wrote to him during the summer—"enjoy a few months of fun before I graduated." Cross-country—running ten and fifteen miles a day, five miles in competition—was painful, unpleasant, and too demanding, I told him.

Marvin Goldberg's written response was a milestone in my life. He informed me that as I grew older, many matters of life would be "painful, unpleasant, and too demanding." Sooner or later I would develop a pattern of response to such situations. I could develop the habit of quitting or I could learn to bear the pain and inconvenience, doing the hard things anyway for the good of those about me. He warned that dropping out of cross-country might set in motion such a pattern of escape that would follow me for the rest of my life. But to return and to master something that I didn't want to do—and to do it for the good of the team—would be to exercise a more important and healthy pattern of determination.

I followed that advice, and two decades later, Marvin Goldberg's character lesson based on his desire for my long-term growth still follows me every day. Having run cross-country—painfully and unenjoyably—I have faced almost every inconvenient situation ever since with the mental determination that originated those days on the running course: "I did it then; I can do it again!"

The world in which our children live appeals almost solely to the present: own this, do that, be what your friends want. A father is one of the only significant people in a child's life who will take the future into account. Thus, his decisions must always relate to what they are becoming. His view is long-range—"downriver." Sometimes it's a rather lonely position. Not many men think that way.

A third significant key to decision-making is taking into account the effects on other people of things our children wish to have or desire to do. An effective father begins in the earliest years to point out to his children—in the words of poet John Donne—that no man is an island. Everything we say, do, or have affects someone else. Our decisions, our exercise of personal rights, the pursuit of our goals cannot be conducted in a relational vacuum.

The Apostle Paul was eloquent about this subject. He reminded Christians that they should be careful not to be "stumbling blocks" for one another. He was getting at the fact that some decisions are bad because they do not take into account the effect their implementation will have on others—even if they are good for the person making the decision.

Watch children at play in the neighborhood. You will note that some are cruel with their words—criticizing and bullying others into submission, oblivious to the effect on the victim's self-esteem. When Mark first wore braces on his teeth, some of his friends enjoyed riding him about it—until they suddenly had to have the silver in their mouths.

The person who has grown up to dominate people, exploit them, or use them for his own purposes in business or community politics is often a product of a home where life was never evaluated on the basis of good for others. Children can be taught at a very early age to think of others. It is never too early to start or too late to get busy.

A fourth and final criterion for "downriver" decision-making is that of determining *exceptions*. Are we flexible enough to let out the rope on occasion to test our children and see how capable they are to make their own decisions? The foresightful father follows laws and convictions. But he is not rigid.

Recently a movie came to our community and all of my son's friends were going to see it. The social pressure was on, and everyone was talking about having seen the film or going to see it. The rating on the film violated our family's convictions, and the normal decision would have been to say, "No way!"

Gail and I talked for some time about this decision. We felt uneasy about following the regular course. We sensed a confusion of priorities and situations. It seemed to be a time for an exception. We agreed that out of this situation might come a learning experience. I went to Mark and I suggested a solution. We would go to see the film together so that we could talk about it when it was over. He agreed and was quite excited. A few days later we went. It was among the better decisions Gail and I have made.

Mark was repelled by the film. The violence shocked him, and he had a hard time getting to sleep that evening. But in the process of talking the film through, he came to understand why our family had drawn a line—a conviction—in the matter of movies. A valuable year has passed now in which we have never been asked for permission to attend anything but a G-rated film.

Our children know of our convictions about the use of tobacco. But since a large percentage of our population chooses to ignore the obvious facts linking smoking to cancer, they cannot help but become curious about what the experience is that draws people to such a habit. Both their mother and I had told Mark and Kris that they were welcome to try smoking a cigarette anytime they wished to satisfy their curiosity—as long as they would do it in our presence.

The time came when they asked. It was the moment for an exception. I went to the store and bought the smelliest unfiltered cigarettes I could find. On a camping trip we opened the pack and allowed them to light a cigarette. At first they laughed at the ease with which they could puff and blow out the smoke. Then I suggested that they inhale. Once was enough. We had two green-faced children. The rest of the package lies waterlogged in the bottom of a lake. Our children have resolved the smoking problem for at least a few years until they have to make their own adult decisions.

Exceptions cannot be made on every issue of conviction. Exceptions can never be made on the laws of God. But there are times when a father must be sensitive enough to know that he must loosen the lines and give opportunity for experiment and experience. Perhaps it is wise for the canoe to be allowed to tip in quiet waters in order to learn the proportions of disaster if it were to capsize in white water.

There are foresightful fathers; there are impulsive fathers. Jacob, the father of twelve sons, was an impulsive one, and he paid the price on many occasions. One dramatic encounter came on a long overland trip when his daughter, Dinah, was raped by Shechem, the son of a village chieftain in the area where Jacob found himself living temporarily. The Bible says that Jacob did nothing at first until his sons returned from tending the cattle. Apparently having no game plan of his own, he allowed his sons to take the situation into their hands. They had no long-range or relational criteria by which to make the decision either. They simply pounced. Shrewdly they plotted retaliation, and in a violent confrontation they killed every male and plundered everything of value in the village.

Only after it was all over did Jacob appear to offer a value judgment. "You have brought trouble upon me by making me odious to all the inhabitants of the land . . . my numbers are few, and if they gather themselves against me and attack me, I shall be destroyed, both I and my household" (Genesis 34:30ff.).

This is not effective fatherhood; it is not foresightful leadership. It is a man acting by impulse and letting everything get out of control. In the end, all Jacob seems to know about the future is that his sons have made a bad mistake. But he has himself to thank. He didn't think through the laws, the convictions, the possibilities. He didn't make a good foresightful decision. Jacob goes down in history as a father who loved his sons but never did quite right for them. He had no foresight.

As Mark and I feel the white water tug at the bottom of our canoe and draw us downstream, I keep my eyes turned forward, picking out the route. If I don't, there will be panic in a few seconds, and we'll be in the water again. We can't afford such mistakes. He knows it and I know it. I wonder if he fully appreciates the same principle when it is in action at home. I know I do, and someday I think he will too.

> It would be so easy, God,
> To make the simple decisions
> That convenience, the desire
> To be liked,
> And momentary peace
> Dictate.

> But just as I withdraw the hand
> Which offers pain, adversity,
> And exhaustion, You remind me
> That one never learns, never grows,
> Never blooms when things are easy.

> Teach me, therefore, God
> To think with eyes and ears,
> To brood with a heart just like
> Yours—
> Which sees things in the scope
> Of Eternity's process: what makes
> People become like your son,
> Christ.

> The ecstasy of this one moment
> —When simple decisions bring
> Temporary tranquility—
> Is not to be compared with the
> Maturity of all the tomorrows
> Through which we must live.

FOURTH PRINCIPLE

If I am an effective father . . .

it is because

I am filling my children's lives with perspectives and patterns which produce wisdom; I am lovingly purging their lives of unwholesome influences and tendencies that impede their progress toward maturity.

12

To Raise
a Great
Cathedral

AMONG THE LEGENDS is the tale of a medieval sidewalk superintendent who asked three stone masons on a construction project what they were doing. The first replied that he was laying bricks. The second described his work as that of building a wall. But it was the third laborer who demonstrated genuine esteem for his work when he said, "I am raising a great cathedral."

Pose that same question to any two fathers concerning their role in the family, and you are liable to get the same kind of contrast. The first may say, "I am supporting a family." But the second may see things differently and say, "I am raising children." The former looks at his job as putting bread on the table. But the latter sees things in God's perspective: he is participating in the shaping of lives.

To shape lives: the phrase suggests the sculptor at work, cutting, chipping, chiseling out of "raw material" a beautiful object of art. Is the effective father an artist? If so, what is he trying to create? The technological world might suggest that it is a person of great skill: an engineer, a scientist, an author, a physician, or a craftsman. But *skill* is not a top biblical priority. The God of the Bible makes it plain that fathers are responsible to produce people of deep inner spirit. *Spirit*, not skill, is essential.

When the Old Testament writers wished to portray the highest levels of spiritual development, they highlighted wisdom. When New Testament writers focused on the greatest spiritual objectives, they developed the concept of Christlikeness: living like Jesus Christ. In terms of quality they amount to the same thing. The wise person is like Christ; the Christlike person is marked with wisdom.

Nowhere in the Bible does the human sculpturing process receive greater attention than in the book of Proverbs. Here Solomon and company catalogued the great principles of life. Threaded throughout the chapters is a great mass of advice about how to raise children to become wise.

When Solomon wanted to point out the virtues of wisdom, he personified it. Thus, he quotes wisdom as saying,

> For whoever finds me (wisdom) finds life and wins approval from the Lord. But the one who misses me has injured himself irreparably (Proverbs 8:35, 36).

The message for fathers is simple: use those tools of fatherhood which introduce wisdom into the lives of your children because wisdom brings one's life to its fullest potential. Ignore those tools which develop wisdom in your children, and you may be pointing them toward a life marked with struggles, misjudgments, and empty achievements.

What is this wisdom of which Solomon speaks? It is a capacity of judgment which grows in the spiritual depths of a human being permitting him to use his knowledge, his abilities, and his opportunities in a way designed by God to be fulfilling and satisfying. Give a child such a gift, and you have given him a treasure which far surpasses the inheritances of the world's richest people.

If you analyze wisdom's message in Proverbs 8:35 a second time, you discover something else that is implicit in Solomon's view of things. Wisdom is not a natural or instinctive characteristic. We are not born with it. It is something which is first given, then exercised, and finally mastered. It becomes the center of one's life. But achieving wisdom is a process which involves much experience.

The wise person learns self-control. He makes decisions based on long-range perspective. He is sensitive to the real issues of human and heavenly relationships. He understands the purpose of his life and how to use the materials of creation to achieve that purpose. He's aware of his weaknesses and how they can be exploited by others, so he carefully avoids such possibilities. Finally, he knows how to serve people, and he hungers to relate to the Living God. Who of us would not like *to raise* children to be wise?

This then is the question upon which a potentially effective father must meditate: what does it mean to raise children to wisdom and Christlikeness? How is it done?

And when do you know that you've succeeded? Obviously there comes a time when the final product depends upon the will of the child himself. But what efforts does a parent make to increase the chances that his son or daughter will make the right choices and pursue a life of wisdom?

After reading Solomon's thinking on the matter, I am convinced that he is telling us that a parent has three things to give his children in order to provide conditions for wisdom. First, he is deeply concerned that we shape that part of a child which produces both habit and desire. That's what we mean by *training* children. Second, Solomon refers to the necessity of *spiritual conditioning*, the enlarging of one's capacity to act in a wise and Christlike way. Third, Solomon sees the need for *punishment*, a way of confronting the child with the consequences of living unwisely. Develop those functions of fatherhood and effectiveness will be dramatically increased.

"Do it again...and again...and again...and..."

Ask Solomon and he'll tell you that adult behavior is largely dependent upon childhood training. "Teach a child to choose the right path," he wrote, "and when he is older he will remain upon it" (Proverbs 22:6). Centuries later the finest minds in the university faculty decided that Solomon's insight was valid. They began to realize that most of a person's adult character and personality is molded before the age of nine. What they're saying is that the seeds of values and choices in the thirties and forties are planted in the first eight years.

In one way or another, almost every page of this book has had something to say about the matter of teaching and training children. A father trains by being a model, by carefully instructing his kids on the job, by giving opportunities for his children to try it themselves. Every moment of relationship between father and children is a part of the training process.

In this never-ending exercise we actually create a complex personality system of habits, reflexes, values, and ambitions. We do it because we have been on the job day and night. My friend the physical therapist understands this process when she works with the paralyzed limb of a patient in the hospital's PT ward. Her experience has been that one can bring a useless limb to action by constant manipulation and exercise. It is impressive to watch her restore the use of arms and legs to victims of stroke or terrible nerve and muscle damage. And she does it in much the same way we train children: constant repetition of certain physical actions.

Something like that happens when we train our children. We do so by repeatedly exposing them to experiences—like the manipulation program of the therapist—which little by little become internalized, automatic, and habitual. Among the first things we train children to do is to sleep at certain times, to recognize certain family personalities, and to develop the proper bathroom habits. Basically, we use these tools: repetition, affirmation, and reinforcement. Sound habits are formed and reflexes trained which make a person progress to maturity.

As a child I lived near a busy avenue which I was strictly forbidden to cross. Naturally, curiosity burned and I always seemed to discover new reasons why I'd like to see and explore the other side of the street.

On that other side were the stores where my mother daily did her shopping. As I grew older, she gradually prepared me for the day I could make the crossing and do that shopping for her.

The first phase of training was the teaching that the

street was a potentially dangerous place. She built into me a healthy respect for the fact that a kid could get killed if he wasn't careful. Until she had convinced me of that fact, all other training was relatively useless. Finally, I believed.

The second phase of training involved crossing day after day, holding my mother's hand. I watched her study traffic patterns and make the right decision each time. This went on for a couple of years until I learned that the proper method could bring one across that big bad street with little trouble.

Mother was shrewd; in time she had me leading her by the hand while I made the street-crossing decisions. For a child this was big business, and I responded to the "heavy" responsibility with enthusiasm. Sometimes I made an unwise decision, and she was there to show me what had gone wrong. When we completed that phase, it was time to move on.

Phase four involved my crossing the street alone while Mother stood at the curb and told me when to go and when to return. Proudly, I would enter the store by myself, purchase bread and milk, and then recross the avenue under her watchful eye.

When further expansion of the training process was possible, Mother simply stood at the front door of our home and watched me make the proper decisions. But I knew that I had arrived when the day came that Mother said, "Son, go across the street and get me a quart of milk." Graduation Day! Mother no longer held my hand, stood at the curb, or even watched from the door. She knew I could handle it. But even then, she would always yell in motherly fashion as I ran out the door " . . . and be careful!" That's training!

In the third chapter of Proverbs, the writer put the objectives of training in another way:

Have two goals, wisdom—that is, knowing, and doing right—and common sense. Don't let them slip away, for they will fill you with living energy, and are a feather in your cap. They keep you safe from defeat and disaster and from stumbling off the trail. With them on guard you can sleep without fear; you need not be afraid of disaster or the plots of wicked men, for the Lord is with you; he protects you (3:21-26).

Within the matrix of these biblical objectives—wisdom, godliness, and even common sense—we raise children. And what do we train them to do? Perhaps the most obvious thing is that we train them to develop proper habits and reflexes.

Habits are daily activities which become so commonplace that we no longer have to think deliberately about doing them. They are there because we've done them repeatedly. Orderliness can be a habit if it is emplaced within a child's mindset early enough. The habit of rising early in the morning is another. Helping around the house, study habits, habits of dependability and consistency are habits we can press into the grain of our children's personalities early in their lives.

Reflexes, on the other hand, are forms of automatic behavior in response to situations around us. We help our children become peacemakers rather than warriors; we train them to hold their tempers when others feel free to retaliate. Matters of common courtesy fall under the dual heading of habit and reflex. It happens because we consistently repeat desirable actions until they are an automatic way of life. Our children see us do them, appropriate the patterns for themselves, and finally internalize them as part of their lives.

We train children on an even deeper level when we

teach values. By our own behavior and by consistent instruction, we teach our kids how to make wise choices. It is only in the first few years that we can totally control our children's moral environment. After that, we must depend upon the soundness of criteria by which they make decisions for themselves.

My children tell me of a boy in their school whose father holds back no material thing from his family. In awed tones Mark and Kris describe the swimming pool, the mobile telephones, the video tape recorders, the vacation trips to Hawaii and Bermuda. At first I feel defensive that I can't provide all these things which seem to make my children envious.

But later at a school function I watch the boy whose family has "everything." I see him stick his leg out to trip another boy as he goes by. I watch him hit a girl on the arm. And I notice how he talks incessantly, always trying to be the center of everything, getting attention in any way possible. I realize that, after all, his father hasn't given him everything. He may outpoint us all when it comes to providing his family with fun and frills, but he is tragically far behind when it comes to giving his children wisdom.

What impresses me is the difference between my scale of values and that of my children. In their immaturity they are impressed with the family which enjoys an unlimited flow of material objects and pleasurable opportunities. We look at the same boy; they see "blessing" while I see approaching disaster.

It all reminds me that I have a long way to go in this business of fatherhood before my children's value structure is built on the proper criteria of judgment. When they begin to evaluate a person's blessings in terms of spiritual and relational capacity, I will know that the training process has reached its goal.

Finally, we train children when we help them shape their ambitions, their sense of personal destiny. Training in this third dimension is not primarily involved with what kind of a career a child is going to follow when he grows up. Rather, let's think about the self-esteem a father gives to his children, which in turn makes them conscious of the potential contributions they can make in the world.

Urging children to reach out and give help to others may serve to stimulate their ultimate interest in being a physician, a pastor, or a counselor. Directing a child's interest toward the fantastic opportunities of discovery in our world may provide direction toward science or engineering. Highlighting a son's or daughter's creativity may lead them toward a life in the arts. But it all begins with our ability to high-profile their sense of self-esteem —their conviction that they are worth something and can make a contribution.

It becomes increasingly important for them to be aware that God wants to use their lives to make a significant impact on society. How many children hear their fathers pray for their future? Do we impress upon them the daily imperative of seeking the wisdom of God's Spirit to make sound decisions? It is not unwise to teach a healthy fear of making mistakes in planning for the future. Life is simply too precious to be wasted.

If we have implanted these habits and reflexes, these qualities of character, and this self-value deep enough, we can relax—assured that we have taken the first step in bringing our children toward a life grounded in wisdom. We have trained them, and set their feet on a way from which they will probably not depart when the going gets rough. At least that's the way Solomon saw it. Teach them again . . . and again . . . and again.

Pain makes the person

There is no record of an inauguration ceremony but you can be sure that there was a tremendous amount of pomp and circumstance the day that Joseph, the son of Jacob, assumed the office of Prime Minister of Egypt. In his early thirties, Joseph had hardly had time to get his eyes used to the light after some years in the darkness of a prison. But here he was in the spotlight, given the number two power-position in the world's strongest nation.

The decision to make Joseph the top man had been made a few days before. The Pharaoh of Egypt had come to grips with the prophetic fact that his nation was facing a tumultuous future. Through Joseph's interpretive abilities, the king had realized that it would take enormous wisdom and power to plan and enforce laws that would conserve Egypt's grain during the coming harvest so that it could be doled out later when famine hit. What kind of a man is it who can persuade a nation to conserve in times of plenty so that they will not starve in times of want?

That's what the Pharaoh asked when he queried his cabinet: "Where can we find a man to do something of this magnitude?" The answer was not long in coming: the man was Joseph.

> "Since God has revealed to you the meaning of the dreams, *you are the wisest man* in the country! I hereby appoint you to be in charge of this entire project. What you say goes through all of the land of Egypt. I alone will outrank you." (signed)
> Pharaoh

Question: Through what process did Joseph get the wisdom? It is not helpful to say simply that it came from

God. We must go beyond that and talk about God's process of giving Joseph wisdom. You will have to trace
your finger across a long line of experiences which built
resilience into Joseph's life.

When Joseph stepped into the Prime Minister's job, he
was *a trained man*. He had acquired managerial experience during his time in the house of Potiphar, an Egyp-
tian businessman. He had enhanced that capability by
rising to the top of the prison administration when he
was thrown in jail on a trumped-up charge. But something more than training was going on at the same time.
Joseph was being *disciplined*. That, in part, was where the
wisdom was growing, for wisdom cannot grow without
discipline.

When a father disciplines his children, he is enlarging
their capacity to endure and produce. To put it in another way, to be disciplined is to be conditioned to performance. The athlete pushes his body to the outer limits of
its capacities until he is utterly exhausted. Why? Because
he wants to be prepared for the race. He wants the run
to be a pushover, relatively easy because he has trained
so hard.

When Joseph took the oath of office, he had a past. He
had faced the painful betrayal of his brothers, the terrible
temptations thrust upon him by Potiphar's wife, and the
agony of being forgotten by close friends who had been
sprung from jail, leaving him to rot. For up to fifteen
years, Joseph faced a constant series of crises. Had he
caved in at any time during that process of conditioning,
he would never have made it to the top. You could say
that an entire nation was saved from horrible catastrophe
because one man had spent the first thirty years of his life
being disciplined to perform when the heat was on.

There must have been many times while in office,
when Joseph was approached by people offering expan-

sive bribes and personal opportunities. He must often have been attacked with brutal criticism. In lonely moments he must have wondered who his real friends were. But the destructive impact of those crises was lessened because he had faced these kinds of challenges before and knew how to deal with them.

There is pain in conditioning, preparation for performance, and there must be pain in the lives of children if they are going to be ready for the challenges facing them. Out of the conditioning experience will come the kind of wisdom that qualified Joseph for his place in the destiny of a nation.

The words discipline and punishment are often used interchangeably. Sometimes it is hard to distinguish between them. I am convinced, however, that there is an important difference. Discipline is the deliberate stress we introduce into our children's lives to stretch their capacities for performance. But punishment is the painful consequence which is the result of misdeeds and violations of family standards and principles.

As I mentioned previously, we started our children working around the house at a very early age. Both Gail and I were impressed with what we had seen among farming families where work was a part of life even among the smallest children. In our suburban home, work appeared to be less necessary. The kids did not really have to participate to keep the family machine going.

That is why we constructed a list of jobs which they began to do at the age of four. We wanted them to experience fatigue, inconvenience, frustration, and puzzling problems. Face problems now, or you'll face them later, we said. But in reality we didn't give them a choice; they were going to face them now. That is a form of discipline.

Discipline helps children learn that feelings do not run their lives. Fluctuating moods, fatigue, ignorance, and even some types of pain will limit us to substandard performance if we allow them to do so. So a wise father, keeping this in mind, attempts to help his children understand that they can push through these barriers and increase their abilities and capacities.

Kristi and I go for a long bicycle ride in the country. We find ourselves pedaling up a much longer hill than we'd anticipated. As we near the top she cries out in fatigue, "I've got to stop and walk." Something tells me that she can probably push on to the top if I encourage her enthusiastically. "I'm positive you can make it," I call to her. "Keep pedaling even if it hurts a little." When she protests a minute later, I point out to her that we're just about there. "Only a few hundred more feet," I yell. She keeps on pedaling, and she makes it.

She is definitely tired, and her legs ache more than they've ever ached before. It was my prodding that kept her going, and now she is glad. The exhilaration of knowing she conquered the challenge is enhanced by the wind at her back as she coasts down the other side. I have added one more nail to the structure of her inner spirit which says, "I can do many things my feelings tell me I cannot do!" That is the development of discipline.

I see opportunity for discipline arising when the kids ask for a ride to school because the temperature has dropped a few degrees, or when they want to buy something that costs a dollar more than they have and they need to borrow it from old Dad. I see it when they keep procrastinating on projects which ought to be done now. So I say, "Walk!" And I say, "Wait!" And I tell them, "Do it now!"

Who wouldn't want to have a son like Joseph? But few would permit their children to face the kind of pain that

Joseph had to endure. Most of us instinctively fall into the trap of withholding the pain, making life relatively easy for our children. I never would have believed how subtle is the temptation to give our children money and freedoms rather than hurt or disappoint them. I had always anticipated that that part of fatherhood would be simple. It isn't! Like most dads, I don't like to see my children hurt, disappointed, and embarrassed because they can't do everything the other kids are doing. I don't like to see them frustrated, facing problems difficult to solve without any help. But then I begin to remember that God must not find it easy to watch us make our way through the stresses of life. He could remove pain in an instant. But he doesn't! In each experience he is helping his children become more like what he wants us to be: like his Son, Jesus.

Wisdom belongs to the disciplined person whose capacities for performance have been enlarged. When the day of the race arrives, the disciplined child steps confidently to the starting line. There will be no backing down from the challenge. He's done it before, he can do it again.

It really does hurt me more than it hurts you

It was a rainy night in Los Angeles, and I was at the airport along with thousands of others, waiting for delayed airplanes to take off. Everyone was obviously tired and irritable. But in the midst of our mutual frustration an episode occurred that saddened all of us.

A young couple had been staring intently out of the observation windows looking for a plane that was—like all the others—late in arriving. So preoccupied were they that their three-year-old daughter wandered off unnoticed. When both mother and father finally turned to see where she was, they became hysterical. Rushing in all directions at once, they began to shout the girl's name. They were frantic, and everyone quickly caught the sense of panic.

It took a few minutes and several airline attendants to locate the child. We were all relieved. But when she was brought to her father, he immediately seized her and began to beat her angrily. At the same time he shouted humiliating and embarrassing threats concerning the consequences should she ever wander off again.

If the furious spanking had continued much longer, I think several of us would have intervened. What stopped us at first was our realization that a parent has a right to punish a child. But the question that was circulating in a lot of our minds as we looked on was this: *is this punishment?* I suspect that we were seeing an uncontrolled man giving vent to his own rage at being exposed as an irresponsible father. Ironically, the child was receiving the pain, but perhaps the father was actually punishing himself.

I remember that situation every time I have to punish our children. Is what I am doing really punishment? Or am I simply taking out my frustrations upon someone smaller than I—someone who won't fight back . . . at least for now. It could be that the punishment is actually vengeance or just anger that I have been let down by my kids.

No subject in the area of child development is more controversial than that of punishment. Naturally, we have the extremes: those who claim that there is no place for punishment and those who see cause for punishment in every untoward act a child does.

If you turn to Scripture, you'll discover that biblical punishment has several different objectives and patterns.

Corrective punishment is meant to warn someone going in
the wrong direction. *Judicial punishment,* on the other
hand, symbolizes the satisfaction of justice when society
has been wronged and the law of God offended. It is also
employed to remove someone who proves to be a destructive element within a group of people.

Jonah is an example of the first kind: *corrective punishment.* God had laid upon his shoulders a special commis-
sion to preach to the people of Nineveh. When Jonah
decided to disobey God, he boarded a ship going in the
opposite direction. It wasn't long before God had Jonah
overboard and in the belly of a great fish.

Jonah's description of the experience is quite vivid:

> (God) threw me into the ocean depths; I sank down
> into the floods of waters and was covered by (his)
> wild and stormy waves. Then I said, "O Lord, you
> have rejected me and cast me away . . . " I sank
> beneath the waves and death was very near. The
> waters closed above me; the seaweed wrapped itself
> around my head. I went down to the bottoms of the
> mountains that rise from off the ocean floor. I was
> locked out of life and imprisoned in the land of
> death . . . (Jonah 2:2-6).

Jonah's three days in the whale are a form of corrective
punishment. It was designed by God to bring him to a
point of submission, a realization of his responsibility. It
appears to be a principle in God's dealings with people
that he will cause pain in our lives in order to call our
attention to mistakes we are making. He does it because
he loves us and seeks our best.

That's why the writer of the Hebrews pictures God as
a father who must sometimes punish his children:

My son, don't be angry when the Lord punishes you. Don't be discouraged when he has to show you where you are wrong. For when he punishes you, it proves that he loves you. When he whips you, it proves that you are really his child (Hebrews 12:5, 6).

There are times when a father—like God—must inflict pain because he wants to high-profile the bad consequences which await a person who continues on the wrong path.

Judicial punishment emerges in the Bible when someone deliberately lives in violation of God's laws. That's what happened to Cain. He rejected God's warnings and, unlike Jonah, he followed through with his own rebellious plans to eliminate Abel. Punishment was swift, and Cain was marked for life because he had rejected God's corrective warnings. The same thing happened to David, king of Israel. As a result of his sin of adultery with Bathsheba, he lost his newborn son in death. These were painful consequences to rebellious acts.

Judicial punishment can be drastic. Sometimes a person appears to be so destructive an influence that he must be removed. You have the Old Testament story of Achan being executed because of his direct disobedience to God. There is the New Testament story of the death of Ananias and Sapphira in the early church for their attempt to "lie to the Holy Spirit." Both of these experiences seem to center on the problems created by people whose continued life in the community of God's people would have been a spiritually cancerous influence. There must be surgery.

Perhaps the most impressive and relevant passage on judicial punishment, however, is that found in Deuteronomy 21:18:

If a man has a stubborn, rebellious son, who will not obey his father or mother, even though they punish him, then his father and mother shall take him before the elders of the city and declare, "This son of ours is stubborn and rebellious and won't obey; he is a worthless drunkard." Then the men of the city shall stone him to death. In this way you shall put away this evil from among you, and all the young men of Israel will hear about what happened and be afraid.

This shocking directive deserves some deep thought. Remember that at the time it was written, the people of Israel were on the move toward the promised land. The rigors of that journey demanded the utmost discipline and orderliness from everyone. There was no time or opportunity for the nation to dissipate its energies coaxing and cajoling dissidents. Thus, the law provided that if a young man would not keep the law, he would have to be punished by execution.

While we do not advocate the "stoning" of children today, there are some valuable principles to be extracted from this passage. The first and foremost fact about the verse is that a family, then and now, cannot easily cope with rebellion. I have watched many parents try to keep their home running happily and efficiently while one child slashed away at the rules whenever they were an inconvenience to him. The home cannot survive under such conditions. This Deuteronomy passage recognizes that and arranges for the final removal of one who disrupts the family.

A second important fact in this verse is that God appears to be recognizing that sometimes children and parents have to part ways if the child decides to reject his parents and their style of life. Jesus indicates this in the parable of the prodigal son. Here is a boy who has apparently received every opportunity his father could provide. I don't think I am making the parable say more than is there when I note that the father seems to have been a good father. But he had a son who couldn't live with the family system. When the boy asked to leave, his father reluctantly let him go. It had to happen. The father could have chained the boy down, but he would never have captured his spirit. Better to surrender the boy to the consequences of his decisions and hope that somewhere along the line the escalating forms of punishment would have an effect. The boy might find correction through consequences. But one thing was sure: as long as his rebellious attitude stayed, he had to go.

On a few occasions when an older teenager has flagrantly violated the family rules and brought heartbreak to his parents and negative influence to the younger children, I have used the Deuteronomy passage to demonstrate a father's right to a drastic solution. The Old Testament verse forces a child to leave; the New Testament principle urges a father to let him leave. By force or by voluntary act, a totally rebellious son or daughter may have to leave his home. If it comes to a question of the family's survival, the interest of the group must take precedence over the individual.

The agony of such a decision often leaves parents who have invested a lifetime in their son or daughter absolutely drained. They have spent countless hours tracing their own failures, and trying new methods of parental relationship. They may have gone through countless times when it seemed as if there was new hope, only to see it explode in pieces. The ultimate anguish comes when they recognize the need for surgery. Perhaps in the "leaving" there will be consequences which will prompt repentence and renewal. Then they will be called upon

202 † THE EFFECTIVE FATHER

—like the prodigal's father—to open the door, forgive, and restore the relationship.

Solomon, convinced that there is an untamed tiger called rebellion in every young life, wrote much about punishment. He said,

> Discipline your son in his early years while there is hope. If you don't, you will ruin his life (Proverbs 19:18).

Solomon seems to be contradicting the unconscious hope many fathers have that their children will "grow out" of their rebellion as they mature. They won't! If the punishment is not applied early in life, the rebellion will simply take on more and more sophisticated forms until one more family has been torn apart, each member broken and disheartened. The wise old king went on to say, "A youngster's heart is filled with rebellion, but punishment will drive it out of him" (Proverbs 22:15).

Corrective and judicial punishment in the book of Proverbs take two forms. The first is *artificial*, and it is targeted at children. The second is *natural*, and it centers on the upper ages. By artificial punishment, I am suggesting that a father or mother must devise consequences which help a child associate pain or hardship with his misdeed. That is all there is to a spanking. It is a very painful experience which dramatizes the seriousness of the wrong act that prompted it.

Natural punishment, which increases with age, is the obvious consequences which come as the result of wrong or rebellious acts. The consequences of loneliness, starvation, and bankruptcy in the life of the prodigal son were natural.

When I was a small child, my parents took me to a lovely new home to visit friends. While the "big folks" were talking, I quietly slipped into the bathroom and managed to pack the toilet with all kinds of objects that weren't meant to be in there. A flush or two jammed the plumbing and the toilet was out of use until it could be repaired.

It seems absurd to point it out, but for the sake of illustration, let me note that natural punishment would have forced me to pay for my vandalism, not only in terms of money, but also in the embarrassment and humiliation for doing such a dumb thing. But being a child, I had no appreciation for either of those natural consequences. I didn't have the money, and I wasn't particularly embarrassed about the matter because I couldn't appreciate the seriousness of what I had done.

That means that the punishment had to be fitted to suit my situation. While I couldn't understand dollar bills, I could comprehend pain. In fact God seemed to have provided a landing pad on the backside of my body which was easy to reach and had a reasonable number of nerve endings to transfer the message to the "inner me." My father was an impresario at artificial punishment, and I soon got the message—loud and clear. By that I mean he was clear and I was loud!

Every family has its own forms of artificial punishments. The universal one appears to be spanking. If you have any respect for Solomon's wisdom, you won't be able to escape the fact that he believed strongly in the inducement of pain through spankings.

> Scolding and spanking a child helps him to learn. Left to himself, he brings shame to his mother (Proverbs 29:15).

Much controversy has swirled about the use of corporal punishment in the family. Some have decried its "violent" quality; others have feared that it tends to express only a parent's momentary frustration and becomes a convenient way to take out rage on someone else. After all, the child can't fight back . . . until later.

Rather than go to either extreme, it might be better to ask ourselves what forms of corporal punishment are possible. My father used to say that, in the earliest months of his children's lives, he found it wise to use a simple flick of the finger on the backside when he sensed anger or rebellion in the cry of a baby. Anyone who has had experience with babies knows what he means when he says that there are several different kinds of cries and a perceptive parent quickly learns which is which. There are cries of pain, hunger, and anger. The first two are legitimate; the third needs to be checked. A finger flick in the early months is sometimes all that a baby needs to associate rebellion with painful consequences.

As a child grows, corporal punishment takes on an even more important role, probably until the age of eight or nine. By then a child's behavior should have been shaped to the point where this kind of enforcement is no longer necessary. With our children, I tried hard never to spank the children with my hand. We had an object set aside for such use, and it was in a certain part of the house where it was easy to reach. It was not used frequently, but it was always dusted off and ready for action should anyone wish to test the authority in the home.

I am convinced that our readiness to use it, and the effectiveness of it when it was employed, contributed to the fact that it was rarely necessary to reach for it. Somewhere in the age-range of seven or eight the weapon disappeared, either by accident or design. But we never had need of it again anyway.

Except in very early childhood when pain is about the only enforcement process available, I am convinced that spankings should never be impulsive. This is a form of punishment that should be reserved for only certain kinds of violations in a home: disobedience, disrespect, lying, the hurting of someone else. The conditions for its use should be well known to everyone.

When spanking is used as a form of punishment, it should be done by a parent who is in total control of himself. If a father, for example, has a tendency to lose his temper, he should be very careful to cool off before he punishes his children. They should never be left with the impression that they are being punished by an angry parent.

Another form of artificial punishment is *isolation*. As I said earlier, a day in one's bedroom may be an invitation to fun, since most children's bedrooms are equipped with a lot to do. We found that asking our children to stand with their faces in the corner of a room was an enforcement experience. Time passes slowly for a child. Thus, thirty to sixty minutes in a corner with nothing to do but stand there looking at nothing gives considerable opportunity to look back on one's attitude and behavior with regret.

The loss of certain privileges or opportunities becomes meaningful in a few years. Toys left out in violation of cleanup laws can be impounded for a week or two. Denial of a favorite television show is a moderate response to certain kinds of unacceptable behavior.

When the children in our home began to learn how to write, I found that the old-time repetitive writing punishment ("I will not . . . again"—written seventy-five times) was quite helpful. I fashioned a sentence that described the wrongdoing and asked a child to record his repentance enough times to grind the meaning of it into his mind. It gives time to draw out remorse, and may even improve handwriting.

As children grow, this exercise can be expanded by asking for essays which describe the offense and how it can be avoided the next time. All privileges are simply suspended until the essay is completed to the parents' satisfaction.

Punishment becomes more natural as children mature. Now a broken window—shattered out of carelessness—can be paid for out of one's allowance or through extra work to which a value is assigned. The familiar term used by all teen-agers, grounding, may be used as they become involved in a peer culture and schedule. Grounding implies the removal of privileges outside the home when a youngster has violated regulations concerning home-coming time or other forms of outside-the-home behavior. "Grounding" has to be associated with the concept that we remove privileges when a child has proved himself unable to handle them responsibly.

Natural punishment becomes especially distressing when we see our children penalized by people outside our home. Punishments applied by school authorities or even the local police, ought not to be interfered with unless they are unjust. Unfortunate as it may be, it is the best thing in the world for a young boy or girl to see firsthand what happens to someone who rebels against the rules of society. The parent who tries to weaken the effect of this by interceding may be making a big mistake. Surely, loving fathers and mothers should stand with their sons or daughters in times of trouble, but they make a serious error if they try to relieve their offspring of responsibility for their actions.

Whether punishment is corrective or judicial, it must happen if we are to bring our children to the wisdom-way of life. But to make it effective, a father must keep certain rules.

Obviously, a first level rule of punishment would have

to be this matter of *anger*. Compare the statements of two fathers, one of whom says, "You make me so mad I could kill you," and another who says, "What you have done grieves me more than you can ever know; I am upset about your actions."

The former statement implies wrath and anger from one person to another. It leaves scars upon the soul of a child and may even make him wonder if his father will ever forgive him. But the latter is different. Note that it shows that the target of the anger is the actions of the person and not the person himself. Our children should know that we are capable of great disappointment and even anger over their actions—but never over them. This principle is entirely consistent with the biblical assertion that the wrath of God is directed at our sins. But God always loves the sinner. Effective fathers can use that as a precedent.

If a parent cannot punish his children without the anger bursting through, punishment should be avoided until everyone is under control. We cause excessive hurt and even engender hatred when we lose our control.

A second principle of punishment is that of *consistency*. We inflict severe damage on children if our punishment of them is erratic and inconsistent. Here again, a father is often motivated to punish his children on the basis of his level of irritability or inconvenience. One day a child does something of which his father disapproves and he says little more than a sharp word or two. But the next day, he swings into action against the same offense and responds with massive force. The child never knows how his father really feels or how he is going to act. Inconsistent punishment is unjust. If a father is convinced that a certain offense is punishable, then it should *always* be punished. If he waffles on some occasions, he destroys far more than he builds.

A third significant principle to remember about punishment is that it *fit the person.* Each child in a family will respond to different forms of punishment, and fathers and mothers have to know these differences. There can be great variations within a single family. One child is crushed over a simple statement of disappointment from his father or mother. But another child will have to be severely reprimanded or spanked before the same message gets through. We have to search for those forms of correction which have the desired effect—no more, no less.

Not only must the punishment fit the person, it must *fit the misbehavior.* An undiscriminating father blows his top at everything. Every violation—whether caused by mistake or rebellion—is met with furious shouting and massive punishment. He doesn't measure the situation and prepare a controlled response which guides his children's lives toward wisdom. Little by little, they come to fear him as an obstacle and an enemy. He has lost their respect.

We have all seen fathers who grounded their teen-aged children for weeks at a time for apparently trivial reasons. They may have been revealing their own fear that the family situation was escaping their fatherly control. But in the long view of things they may cause a far more serious alienation than the immediate positive correction.

Two more principles of punishment were impressed upon me when I watched a father blow his top over something his son was doing. He grabbed the boy violently and proceeded to spank him. When he stopped—out of sheer exhaustion—the boy had not yet responded. In fact, as the father walked away in disgust, I saw the boy grin and heard him say to a friend of his, "It didn't really hurt a bit."

The father's first mistake was punishing his son in public, and you can note that as my fourth principle of punishment. We punish our children *in private*—never in front of anyone, including other members of the family. Punishment is not meant to humiliate; it is to restrain the destructive will. It should be between only two people: a parent and the child. No one else should ever be present.

The father's second mistake was a violation of my fifth principle: he wasn't thorough. A spanking which does not bring a change of attitude and spirit is worse than no spanking at all. You can hardly ever go out in public without seeing some mother or father casually reach out and swat a child. The child will often show no reaction. All the parent has done is to change the situation for a few minutes. But with a succession of such ineffective punishments comes an immunity to all punishment. The boy who says to his friends, "It didn't hurt a bit," is actually saying, "Hey, I can beat the system."

Ineffective punishment in childhood can develop an unhealthy attitude toward the natural punishments of later years. If there is no ultimate fear of any kind of punishment, there is no deterrent to rebellion. With no deterrent, you can expect the willful spirit to produce a chamber of horrors and heartbreaks.

I have a sixth principle of punishment, and like the seventh, it is distinctly Christian. Punishment must have *a beginning and an ending.* It begins when a father informs his child as to why he is being punished. If both parent and child have not come to an understanding of what the violation has been, then the punishment has no meaning. That's why it is often important to wait until anger and frustration have subsided so that both parent and child can fully understand what happened and why it must be treated.

Doing that will insure that a child is not punished unjustly. A child must be given the chance to explain and tell how he feels about what he has done. He cannot always be allowed to apologize his way out of punishment because then he will learn that "I'm sorry" is a passport to freedom every time. Such apologies mean nothing.

Equally important is the fact that when the punishment is ended there is complete forgiveness and restoration. Among the many traits I admire most about my father is the fact that once I had been punished, he never held any of my past misbehavior against me or reminded me of previous punishments. I could be sure that when a matter had been concluded in private, it was ended forever. He would hold me in his arms until I finished crying and then would establish a fresh fellowship between us. Perhaps that is why I never held a grudge against either of my parents.

That principle is distinctly Christian because it involves forgiveness. And forgiveness in the biblical context means that something is never again held against us. It may perhaps be a while before we are given a second chance, and it may be a while before total trust can be built up again. But in the broadest sense, a deed once punished must then be forgiven. Children must be taught in the context of punishment the necessity for repentance and the resulting forgiveness. Here in this crucible of pain, they may learn some of the greatest relational lessons of life.

The final principle of punishment that seems to encompass all of the others is this: punishment emanates *from a heart of love*—not vengeance. What did Mother and Dad mean when they used to say, "I punish you because I love you and want you to grow to be a man of God"?

It takes an adult mind to understand the wisdom of that. Or does it?

Kristen describes to me a home in which she has recently visited. In a matter-of-fact commentary on her experience she says, "I don't think they love their children very much, Dad."

That comment fascinates me, and I pick it up. "What makes you think that, Kris?" I ask.

Very thoughtfully she responds, "Well, they never say 'no' to their children, and they never get mad at them for anything. They just let them do anything they want."

I know that I am hearing something special, and I maintain the conversation's momentum. "But I thought that was the way you'd like to have parents act. Think of it: no one bossing you around; no one ever punishing you; no one every stopping you from doing anything you want. I thought that's the way you wanted things to be."

"It may be the way we sometimes want things to be," she responds, "but it's not what's best for us. Grownups know best what we need because they love us. Someday we'll know too." Kristen is on to something valuable. She has realized that punishment—effective punishment which brings wisdom—comes from a heart of love.

Since this is a book about fathers, I've talked about punishment from the fatherly perspective. But I don't mean to imply that mothers are not responsible for punishment in the home. A home is in danger if either parent leaves the punishing of children totally up to the other.

It would seem wise for mother and father to agree upon a punishment policy. Children will quickly learn if one of them is softer than the other. I learned that one time when Kristi was quite young. She was about to be spanked by her father, and she cried out, "Daddy, please let Mommy spank me." She knew there was a difference. We leveled out the differences quickly.

Where misbehavior has been serious, then it may be advisable for the father and mother to talk over the situation before any kind of punishment is carried out. In our home, I have taken the responsibility of handling major situations. This would seem to be the responsibility of the head of the family.

The days of artificial punishment are almost over in our house. We will never spank again, and I am glad. It always did hurt me more than it hurt them. We've entered the era of natural consequences. And should our children choose to violate God's laws and society's rules, they will suffer. If that happens, we will suffer with them. My prayer is that we brought just enough *corrective* enforcement to bear so that we taught them an abiding fear of stepping out of the way of wisdom.

A friend of mine tells of a time when he was out of the country. This young Christian had been alone for many days, and he was confronted with the temptation to see a pornographic movie. Curiosity and distance from home were two strong convincing factors as he wrestled with the temptation. Standing there in front of the theater, he recalled a hymn his parents had taught him many years before:

> I would be true, for there are those who trust me.
> I would be pure, for there are those who care.
> I would be strong, for there is much to suffer.
> I would be brave, for there is much to dare.

The reminder of those words and the truth they represented caused my friend to walk on to his hotel room with a pure heart. A moment of truth had occurred, and because the right patterns had been instilled through training, discipline, and punishment, he was able to perform. The decision was a wise one.

For many, my friend's decision seems to be a minor one compared to the long haul of life. But Joseph's decision not to quit when rejected by his brothers, or not to give in—even once—to Potiphar's wife, or not to grow resentful when forgotten in prison could have been considered minor decisions also. But in each case he made the right one—the wise one. And the chain of wise decisions led straight to the most powerful office in the land.

That is what an effective father does. He doesn't support a family; he raises it. The harvest appears when a child has grown into wisdom of life and Christlikeness of behavior. In the final analysis, we seek not to raise children of skill but children of the spirit. That's what God wants.

FIFTH
PRINCIPLE

If I am an effective father . . .

it is because

I accept and affirm my children for who they are, appreciate them for what they are accomplishing, and cover them with affection because they are mine.

13

Please
Show Me
That You Care

THE ANNUAL PTA sixth-grade play had just ended. The gymnasium had been packed beyond capacity, the air stuffy, and the show thirty minutes longer than expected. But since we the audience were all parents, we overlooked the negatives and preferred to dote on the evening, convinced it was an Academy Award-level performance. When the principal dismissed us, we began to gather in small groups for the usual friendly chatter.

It was in that setting that I witnessed a tiny post-show drama that had absolutely no significance for anyone except a twelve-year-old girl and her father. She had played a minor role in the program and now she had come from backstage to find her parents, obviously anticipating their response to her on-stage achievements. When she spied her father talking to another man, she cried, "Daddy, Daddy" and ran to grab his hand.

She was still jumping up and down in the expectancy of his reaction to her part in the play, when he said sharply, "Barbie, don't interrupt me! Can't you see that I'm talking to Mr. Mathewson? I'll be through in a minute."

I may have been the only one who saw it, but it was clear to me that the light in the child's eyes was immediately extinguished. The message received had been blunt and—under the circumstances—quite cruel: "Your performance was not as important to me as my interest in what my grown-up friend is saying."

Approval by significant people in our lives is a fundamental need. Our composite health—physical, emotional, and spiritual—cannot survive without it.

When one speaks about this kind of need, the emphasis is not upon superficial applause but rather something which God built into each one of us at creation. The Christian is promised that if he has faithfully served his God, one day he will hear from his Heavenly Father the acknowledgment "Well done, good and faithful servant." The Bible includes teaching on the doctrine of heavenly rewards which we should not be ashamed to keep in mind as we serve.

In the meantime God has created us to need lesser but still significant forms of approval from the principal people in our lives: our parents, our spouses, our close friends, even to some extent the general community about us. We need it badly, and if we don't get it, we die a little bit inside each day. In short: we all flourish or wither in life depending to a great extent on God's approval, the approval of others, and finally our approval of ourselves.

A twenty-six-year-old man comes for a conversation with me and begins to outline a personal struggle with inferiority, something with which he has wrestled for years. It doesn't take long to get to the point of his relationship with his father. We trace a consistently disappointing boyhood experience on those occasions when the father noticed something his son had accomplished. Whether it was school work, an athletic victory, a model plane, or an attempt to do a job around the house, the response was uniformly the same: *dissatisfaction and criticism*—"You could have done it better . . . faster . . . easier." The father seemed impossible to please.

Under those circumstances most children will make an indefinite number of attempts to please their fathers, always hoping that next time the response will be different. But if nothing changes, the result is usually a growing mental habit pattern called *low self-esteem*—the personal conviction that one is useless and worthless.

As I visit with my new friend, I realize that unless someone can convince him that his father was insensitive and blind to what he was doing to his son, he is apt to go through life convinced that his father's view of his capabilities was correct. He will be a "self-styled loser" in everything he attempts.

So strong had been this kind of childhood input that it had not only shaped all attitudes and approaches to work, but it devastated his view of himself as a whole person. The young man ceased to pursue any form of excellence because he had been inadvertently trained by his father to think that it was impossible to achieve. Finally, he came full circle to the point where he unconsciously agreed with his father's opinion. As I talk with him, my mind snaps back to the little girl at the PTA presentation. Is this what she is going to become? Does her father's devastating rebuke represent a pattern that is often repeated in her life?

The failure of the child to gain approval from his father causes my friend to wrestle with low self-esteem. He could have found himself the victim of other kinds of problems. He had chosen a personality style of *withdrawal and retreat*. Others with his kind of background have moved in a different direction. They may be the adults we meet who have an insatiable appetite for prominence and recognition. They cannot rest until they are president, the chairman, the biggest, the best, or the richest. They must win and win decisively.

Recently I visited with a physician who specializes in the treatment of migraine headaches. He shared his frustration over the fact that there are no known causes for most types of migraine headaches. What has caught his interest, however, is that the overwhelming number of patients he treats are high achievers, the men and women who have to win at everything they do. In his consultations he discovered that a great majority of them had experienced poor relationships with their fathers in the area of approval. One man in his early sixties, enormously wealthy and vested with incredible corporate power, admitted that he was still trying to please the father of his childhood. The pressure never seemed to disappear. Result: a routine of life marked with migraines, ulcers, and heart disease.

I am thinking of these two classic reactions—withdrawal and overachievement—when I say good-bye to the young man who has come to see me. Before we can schedule another visit at my office, he makes a vacation visit to his aging father. The two of them enter into long conversations, and because he is not sensitized to the root of his problem, he shares some of his pent-up feelings.

His father shudders in mild shock. It had never occurred to him, he responds, that his son felt that way. Didn't the son ever sense how much pride the father really felt in his boy? How had they misunderstood each other so badly? Hours pass by as the father recounts one instance after another in which he had *felt* strong approval and pride in his son.

But that is a major portion of the problem. While he had *felt* pride for his son, the man had never *expressed* it. *Now* it flows forth in words . . . fifteen years after a son's personality is firmly molded. How does a father apologize for cheating his son out of something he can no longer fully restore? The two weep as they attempt to make up for lost time. The father admits that he had always feared that too much approval would soften the boy's will to push ahead. Fortunately, he now sees that he went to a dangerous extreme.

The young man who comes to see me after that vacation visit is a person in the process of healing. He has heard a kind of earthly "well done" and though it will be several years before he can break the habit of seeing himself from a sub-par perspective, a breakthrough has occurred. He can at least put the past behind him and concentrate on his self-value in the present and future.

I have not described an unusual experience. The only part of it that is unique is that there was some degree of resolution or healing. Many sons and daughters never get to hear from their fathers what my friend finally heard from his. It is also worth noting that in a majority of cases, if approval is not satisfactorily transmitted during the stages of childhood, even the most enthusiastic of endorsements from a parent later on may not fulfill the entire need. Some things bypassed during childhood are never entirely recoverable. In this man's case an unusual exception occurred.

I am convinced that a large part of our personality-style rests upon a chain of significant relationships which follow us through our lives. The first significant relationships, of course, are those with our parents. The next set probably includes brothers and sisters. Certain friendships and authority relationships—schoolteachers, for example—make up a third package. A fourth level moving into adulthood would be that of one's spouse. All of these relationships must be fully resolved and healthy. Resolution probably includes such things as approval, peaceful settlement of conflicts, and a giving and gaining of some important clusters of information and experiences.

Most of our inner struggles are rooted in one or more unresolved relationships—the one with our fathers and mothers being the most important. These must be brought to a peaceful settlement. If not, there will always be some sort of "monster" of irresolution in our inner spirits wanting to stick its ugly head into our consciousness at the most inconvenient time in later years.

This need for approval and resolution is known to continue even after a mother and father are dead. If one is unsure about how his parents really felt about him, he may mentally pursue their approval indefinitely. He may, on the other hand, suddenly call that pursuit to an unconscious end, shove it deep down into the mysterious depths of his inner spirit, and then wonder why he feels strong resentments toward anyone who subconsciously reminds him of his old style of life and authority: a boss, a pastor, a teacher, or even a spouse, for example. He may actually be projecting actual hatred for his dead parents on people who presently exist. This is not an unusual experience. Everyone of us who at one time or other fulfills a role of authority in our little society may experience the brunt of resentment or resistance from someone who is actually seeing in us the pattern of a father or a mother toward whom they have residual hatred or hostility.

These are the possibilities that an effective father must keep in mind as he attempts to maintain the precarious balance between approval and criticism when he relates to his children. So delicate is this parental exercise that he must prayerfully resensitize himself to it every day. It never becomes totally automatic. Approval and criticism must be deliberate, well thought out.

My impression of the average father is that he wishes to express approval and pride in his children. But his problem often seems to be that he finds it difficult to say what he thinks. Perhaps he worries about being too complimentary, or he struggles to convey his sense of satisfaction but uses words which mean little to the child. Slowly he unconsciously falls into the trap of thinking that his children know how he feels, and that is his serious mistake. He must not assume anything.

There are several ways a father extends approval to his children. Call the first of them simply *"verbal affirmation."* Affirming others is the act of expressing how valuable we think they are as persons. We *affirm* people for what they are; we *appreciate* people for what they do. Both are quite necessary.

Affirmation seems to flow quite freely from mothers to children. Usually a child is secure about his mother's opinion of him. Unless she deliberately betrays his confidence in her, a child finds it easy to assume that his mother's love and acceptance is automatic. After all, he subconsciously reasons, she carried me within her, she bore me, and now she takes care of me. She must have positive thoughts about my value.

Not so with his father, the child thinks. Who really knows how dad feels? As far as a child can see, dad isn't really tied into the family situation—at least to the extent that mother is. Dad comes and goes, has responsibilities in other parts of the big world. How does dad feel about us anyway, the child wonders. Obviously, dad's approval will have to be earned. It cannot be assumed. His attention must be caught.

Fathers respond to their children and affirm them in all kinds of ways. Private signals such as winks, gestures, taps on the shoulders, lots of hugs and kisses, here and there a special word: they are all part of the special vocabulary of affirmation. Children learn the language quickly; they know how dad feels; it's obvious to them when he is pleased and when he's not. Once they have this system of communication figured out and know that dad is responsive to their performance as persons, they will do anything to receive a continuing flow of that affirmation.

Imagine then a child's frustration when he discovers that his father doesn't speak the language of affirmation or that the language is not consistent or discernable. It's even worse when a father's language is not marked with affirmation but rather with ridicule, sarcasm, and disgust. Disaster!

As fathers we must know not only how to affirm our children but *when* and for what purposes. Some fathers, for example, express affirmation only in response to things that are personally important to them: athletic achievements are one obvious kind of performance which might illustrate this. It is not unusual for both sons and daughters to learn that the only worthwhile things they can do as children, in terms of their father's approval, are related to winning on the sports field. The records are filled with the mistakes of fathers who made it very plain that their sons could find satisfying acceptance only as athletes. How many times has a boy donned a practice uniform and gone out on the field, but, unable to succeed, has sensed that he's not only failed to make the team but has failed his father. If his father is insensitive enough, it can be a disaster moment in their relationship, because the boy will either sink into low self-esteem or he will finally cease to care what his father thinks. The spectrum of approval has been too narrow. Sports is not enough.

Consider the son or daughter who should be affirmed for things he is genuinely capable of doing, even if they don't match a father's personal interest or expectations. The boy who is artistically inclined rather than able to throw a forty-yard pass; the girl who shows excellence in a school research laboratory, rather than being high scorer on the field hockey team. It is possible that if each senses that a father's approval is to be found only in some other area of interest, they will drop that for which they are best suited and pursue the thing that will gain a father's acceptance. Tragedy!

Herein lies a call to *sensitivity*. What does my child want to do? What does he do best? And where does he need approval? What qualities of character and personality do I see that need to be highlighted and praised so that my children can know that I consider them important? These questions need thoughtful response.

Among the list of needed affirmations is simply the statement "I love you." Over the years I've established a kind of tradition with Mark and Kristen. My "I love you" and their similar response are usually the last words we say to one another each night. We have learned the words at an early age and none of us are ashamed to say them.

It must always be remembered, however, that affirmation and appreciation must be sincere and genuine. Approval of a child's *personhood* should be automatic because they are son or daughter to a father. But approval of a child's *achievements* must be honestly earned so that the resulting endorsement will not seem phony or hypocritical. The need is for a sensitive balance.

A daughter confides to her father that she is worried about not winning an office for which she is running in the school election. "Dad, I want it badly," she says. Among her fears may be the disappointment her father and mother may have that she isn't good enough. She needs to hear her father say, "Honey, the most important thing to me is not whether you are elected. What I care about is that you genuinely represent your own personal standards of excellence. I'll never be disappointed in your defeats if I know that you did your best. I'll be right behind you no matter what the result."

Genuine affirmation is important not only for the momentary feeling of security that it provides, but it opens the gateway to healthy future relationships. A daughter's first attempts to reach across the sex barrier to please men will be with her father. It is from him that she first needs to know if she is attractive, if her conversation is interesting and her creativity worthwhile. If her father applauds her mental and spiritual attributes at an early age, she will learn not to rely solely on shallow qualities like sex appeal to attract other men in her adult years. Affirmation from her father in proper doses will convince her that she is important as a person and not as a sex object.

If her father is perceptive, he will begin early in his daughter's life to let her know how pleased he is with her. He will urge her to copy the admirable traits of her mother. Through approval and affirmation he will constantly highlight her developing capacities. He will point out the achievements of other women who are accomplishing things in the world and he will encourage her to make worthwhile contributions of her own. As she learns to please him in these ways, she will be able to handle herself with confidence among other men as she grows older. Her adult relationships with men will be of an extremely high caliber if triggered by early ones with her father.

There are special situations in life in which affirmation is even more critically important. A child with a weight problem needs affirmation along with help to reduce. Children getting their first braces or eyeglasses may need a bit of compensating affirmation. They may hear the opposite from the more cruel members of their peer group. The clumsiness which sometimes accompanies the onset of puberty can be helped by affirmation. Don't forget the moments of disaster when a daughter loses out on a date or a son is left out of a special group he longs to join. These are the times when the effective father gets to work and reaffirms the worth of his children. His opinion counts, and he must make it known.

As affirmation concentrates on what a child is, *appreciation* highlights what a child has done.

Kristi thinks it is great fun to come to my office and play secretary. Sometimes I get the feeling she thinks her dear old fumbling dad just isn't going to make it without help from her. If I leave the office to her for a half hour, I can be almost positive that she will have rearranged or cleaned or completed something.

One day after she had done a cleaning job on my desk I slipped a piece of stationery into the typewriter and wrote her a formal letter of thanks and put it in the mail. Watching her read it the next day was worth a lot.

Children need to be appreciated for the contribution they make to our lives. Through such expressions of appreciation, they begin to learn that they are not along for a free ride in the family, but that they have valuable contributions to make to the family's welfare. They are a vital part of our family life; we need to tell them so.

It is relatively easy to give the impression that a family is made up of two levels of people: first-class parents and second-class children. The family is not a two-decker society; it is a circle of people dependent on one another. If the former mentality prevails, then the children get the impression that parents are pulling the family wagon along until such a time as the kids are old enough to pile off the top of the load and go on their way. If they have that idea, the problem usually lies in the failure of the parents to convince their children that everyone has to pull the wagon. No pull, no progress!

Perhaps that is one of the reasons Americans are attracted to the Walton family on television. Something warms us about the way each person has a part to play in the lives of the others. The parents cannot get along without the kids, and the kids obviously can't make it without the parents. Not so in most families today. Children too often receive the impression that they are not necessary to the family's functioning.

This is the reason for the importance of a constant flow of gratitude among family members. In the act of appreciating one another we are saying, "You are very important and it would be a stiff struggle to make it without you."

We instituted "appreciation night" a few years ago in our family. At the end of the school year we celebrate by going out to one of the best restaurants. The featured guests are the children; it is a testimonial dinner in their honor. Little thank-you notes, gifts on certain occasions, specially decorated cookies and cakes can be ways of saying, "You've done a great job and we're thankful for you."

The appreciated child is an adjusted child, happy with his place in the family. He is aware that he really counts.

The physical expression of our approval is of great importance. We affirm what a person is, and we appreciate what a person does. But this assurance must be given in more than words. *Affection,* the nonverbal communication of closeness, touching, and stroking is among the most important experiences we share with one another.

A young woman came to talk with me about a marriage problem. As the details spilled out, I listened to a tragic confession of a wife's unfaithfulness and consistent promiscuity. Later we dug deeper and deeper into the past years trying to uncover the roots of a sexual behavior pattern which was almost as much an addiction as alcoholism. We came finally to her memories of her father.

"Did you and your father enjoy a close relationship?" I asked.

"I cannot remember a time when my father so much as touched me," she responded. "In fact, until I was a teen-ager and started going out with boys, I don't remember a time when I was touched affectionately by any man." I think we reached a root cause of her present problem.

Children need the kind of approval which is transmitted physically through touching. The woman who came to talk with me that day had never experienced any of this. It seems incredible that some men have to be challenged with this fact, but apparently many do. The need for physical affection begins at birth. Some suggest that affection may actually be an extension of the prenatal experience, the security which one enjoys when enveloped in the warmth of a mother's womb. We need to be reminded of that total experience of the womb, and it is met to some extent each time we enter into physical proximity with one another.

In the earliest years touching means protection, security, and healing. For a long while nothing will quite equal the importance of receiving physical closeness from father and mother.

One sees the incredible need for touching when a child falls down the stairs or is startled by a crash of thunder. Frightened, he frantically runs to the legs of his mother or father, seeking reassurance and protection.

As a child grows, touching takes on an extended significance. It tends to diminish as a symbol of protection and increases as a symbol of acceptance. Touching says something about specialness: "I invite you into an intimate circle of my life." Somewhere this touching has to happen and if it cannot be found in the home with the proper people, it will be sought from other, possibly less wholesome, sources.

Again it seems axiomatic that most mothers provide an ample amount of affection. Rarely does one talk with women who have trouble giving their children the cuddling they need. The order of life has taken mother and child through the birth experience together. Normally this intimacy continues, changing only in the forms appropriate to each stage of maturity.

But a father can be another matter. If he has not learned the importance of affection toward his children, he may tend to invest affection with sexual implications. If he is ignorant of his children's needs, he shares his affection only with his wife and that on a sexual basis. He considers affection toward his son to be unmanly; he does not feel that it's appropriate to show affection to his daughter.

But an effective father is unafraid of physical expressions of his love. He uses his touch of affection to convey the message of acceptance and love. He never stops.

I found, for example, that my son loves to have his hair tousled and his ears roughed. When he was very young, I discovered that I could get him to sit like a statue in church services simply by running my fingers through his hair. I'm not suggesting that he was getting a lot out of the service, but he certainly learned that a church service could be a time of warmth and closeness to his father. That may be good preparation for the jump he must make in establishing a warm relationship with his Heavenly Father.

My daughter, on the other hand, is the back-scratching type. How memorable the evenings when I have put her to bed and sat at her side rubbing her tiny back. A father who thinks a television show is more important than a child's bedtime will lose out on some of the most wonderful moments of life. He will miss the joy when his daughter takes his face in her two small hands and rubs his day-old beard, studies his wrinkling middle-aged forehead, and kisses the tip of his nose.

Many fathers unconsciously begin to withdraw from their daughters when they notice the first signs of puberty. The hugging, the lap-sitting, and frequent kisses are liable to decline if a father worries about their effect upon his daughter simply because her body is maturing. He doesn't realize that this is the time when she needs him most.

Research reveals that girls who enter into promiscuous sexual relationships at an early age almost always come from homes where fathers have been unaffectionate and have failed to meet the need of their young daughters to be touched and physically affirmed. This fact made me become interested in the father-daughter relationships in the life of that young woman who asked my advice about her problem of marital infidelity. What is the root of her present moral weakness? Why is she unable to restrain herself sexually? What has loosed a stream of sexual dissatisfaction which betrays her today?

My conversation with her must begin somewhere in

this area and so we painfully recall early experiences in which her father had failed to perform. Let me emphasize that it is not my intention in counseling to absolve this woman of her own accountability for her sin. Rather, I seek to help her understand some factors that predisposed her to fall so easily into sexual sin. Here I am exploring a situation which is both theological and psychological. Like any of us, she has not sinned alone. An incomplete parent-child relationship made it more likely that her sin would occur. The harvest is now being reaped some ten to fifteen years later.

This woman's healing process will be slow and painful. There is the embarrassment of facing her situation and admitting what she has become. There is the struggle to face habit patterns of needs and replace them with far sounder patterns of need and behavior. There will be the spiritual battle to experience God's forgiveness and restoration. And there will always be the indelible memories so often left by sin.

I grieve as I help her put the pieces of her life back together again. It takes time and there must be many meetings in the pastor's study. Why must many of us spend our lives doing things the hard way because the normal, healthier ways were ignored in an earlier time? This woman presently battles for a wholesome pattern of life against obstacles which are almost insurmountable. Perhaps the battle would never have existed if she had enjoyed the kind of father relationship she deserved as a child.

As fathers, it is very easy to rationalize why any of us might have made the kind of mistake her father made. I hear some fathers say, "I guess I'm not the affectionate type. My parents were from the old country and they never expressed affection openly, so I never have either." How do we convince men out of this background that this is not "the old country," that this is the day when feelings can and should be conveyed through affectionate touching? How do we convince them that contemporary effective fatherhood *demands* a break with the past? Something different is possible in the present.

How easy it is to ignore our children's need for affection. Impatiently, we shake off the hand they extend when we walk beside them. We feel intruded upon when they suddenly interrupt our concentration, asking for a hug. A father I know had faced a series of such interruptions as he was reading his evening newspaper. He was just about to explode with irritation when a more pleasant alternative crossed his mind. He placed his newspaper on the floor and took his little son into his arms. The transaction of affection lasted for about thirty seconds. Then, satisfied, the child wriggled out of his arms and went back to his play. There followed twenty minutes of uninterrupted newspaper reading. "He was just testing me," my friend recounted. "Normally I would have spent a total of five minutes resisting his interruptions, but thirty seconds was all it took to assure him that I loved him and that I was willing to express it. Why couldn't I realize that more often?" Yes, why?

Affection is more than hugs and kisses. As children grow older their need for affection does not cease, but they may prefer a different way of expressing it. One father tells me that his son passed through a period where he didn't want his dad to kiss him good-night. The father pondered this request and later mentioned it to his son. "I've been thinking about your not wanting me to kiss you good-night. I'm willing to play the game your way, son, but I do need a substitute action. There has got to be some way I can tell you that I love you and that everything is really great between us. If you prefer that I not kiss you, would you accept a squeeze on the shoulder?" The boy saw no problem with that. From that time on the father honored his boy's wishes. He didn't kiss him good-night, but he always squeezed the boy's shoulder. The father never fully comprehended the importance of this until one night when he began to leave the room without extending the usual gesture of affection.

"What's wrong, dad?" his son called after him.

"Why do you ask?" the father wanted to know.

"You know. You didn't grab my shoulder the way you always do."

"You're right, son. I blew it," the father said. He turned back and performed the small rite of affection that both had come to accept as the important expression of love in that phase of the son's life. A father had learned a valuable lesson. What was relatively inconsequential to him had become a very important matter to his son. What if he had missed it? In fact, what if he had originally misinterpreted his son's desire not to be kissed and had forgotten about affection entirely. Listening to his son's superficial feelings about kissing, he would have missed the unspoken statement of a boy's heart: "Dad, I want your affection as much as ever, but during this time of growing up, please convey it to me in a different way." Wise father; satisfied son.

If forms of affection change, so do the appropriate times. Why are many children embarrassed when their parents display affection out in public? Because pride and peer pressure say that they're too old to need such affection. But in fact, they do! So the battle between what is *acceptable* and what is *needed* goes on. Effective fathers can sensitize themselves and simply resolve to give affection as it is needed and wanted. The child may not be mature enough to swallow his pride; presumably a father is.

I keep this in mind when my son comes off the soccer

field and wants only a congratulatory handshake. But I also remember it when a half hour later he is so exhausted that he readily stretches out on the seat of the car and puts his head on my lap and drops off to sleep. As I drive home, my affectionate hand can extend to him all the love, the pride, the affirmation I feel because it is an acceptable time and place. Who else needs to know that he needs it and I desperately want to give it? But we can both wait until "the guys" aren't looking.

The Bible says that Jesus faced an interminable series of busy days. One VIP after another was squeezed into the hours for conversation. There were meetings, confrontations, and training sessions. There were long walks, big decisions, magnificent healings. From the perspective of the disciples it was a major undertaking. This Jesus was an important person—far too important, certainly, to spend much time with mere children. From their shallow vantage point the ministry of the gospel was more significant than kids. Leave them alone and they will grow up; then they can get time with the Lord. That was the disciples' view.

But Jesus saw it differently. On one occasion when the disciples were fresh from debating the issue of who among them was the greatest, Jesus took a child and put him in the midst of them. Wrapping his arms around the little boy or girl, Jesus said, "He who receives this child receives me. . . . " We don't know the child's name or family. All we know is that the Son of God, the Prince of Heaven, was saying that children are incredibly important, first, because they are human beings. They are important because this is the most formative period of their lives. They are important, furthermore, because they need and deserve treatment as the most significant human beings in the world. The disciples took a long time learning that, and so do many fathers. That's a major reason why a large part of the gospel is so frequently misunderstood.

What was Jesus saying? In word and in truth, he was suggesting the obvious: that the atmosphere in which children grow to fullest maturity is marked with affirmation—recognizing what a child is; appreciation—recognizing what a child does; and affection—recognizing ways to show love for a child. For these factors there are no substitutes; in implementing them, there can be no delay.

SIXTH PRINCIPLE

If I am an effective father . . .

it is because

I am aware that I always live on the edge of ineffectiveness and must continually reach out to God for wisdom and skill to accomplish my task.

14

The Sour Hour–
The Ineffective
Father

A WELL-WORN COMEDY routine features a cast of passengers seated in a jetliner which is climbing to its cruising altitude. Over the cabin intercom comes a calm voice notifying everyone that the plane is fully automated; in fact, there is no pilot, no navigator, and no cabin attendants. This "modern miracle of science" is thoroughly dependable because all mechanisms are fail-safe. To further assure the listeners, the taped voice of the plane's computer goes on to say, "Nothing can possibly go wrong . . . go wrong . . . go wrong . . . go . . . "

That is exactly what a lot of young fathers have felt

during the earliest years of their children's lives. At the ages of two and five those children seem much too innocent ever to drift or deviate from the family pattern of life and convictions. But it must be faced: all young people and adults whose lives have turned sour started out being "cute" and "delightful." It seemed impossible then to imagine that something could go wrong. But in thousands of homes every year something does go wrong. The sour hour of rebellion suddenly extends into days, weeks, months—perhaps even a lifetime. Left in the wake of the family mess are fathers and mothers who live with the awful aftertaste of defeat.

What about those moments through which every father and mother pass when they sense total paralysis, the inability to achieve a semblance of success as parents? Are there any families which have not experienced crises when everything seemed to disintegrate? The child a parent thinks he knows so well suddenly appears to reject everything that is important and right. Tension fills the air; sullenness, anger, and distance are the order of the day. "What have I done wrong?" a father asks. "And what do I do now?"

Soon after I had finished the first draft of *The Effective Father* I came to the week of my birthday. When my big day arrived, Gail scheduled a big celebration. From the moment she arose that morning, she was in motion, planning the big party. A few days earlier I had told her that I would prefer to spend the evening at home, with her and the children. We would not go out and we would not invite friends in. She heeded my wishes and she planned a menu of my favorite foods. When I came home the table was set, candles lit, the birthday dinner ready. But the children were not!

The first storm warnings came when I called Mark and Kristen to the table and they did not promptly appear. A favorite TV show was on and they were so engrossed in it that they ignored my call. It took four calls—each progressively firmer—to get them upstairs from the basement. With good humor befitting the birthday-person, I ignored their tardiness and stifled my usual conviction that delayed obedience is disobedience. This is no occasion for confrontation, I thought.

Sign number two came when they entered the dining room and immediately began to complain about the food they saw on the table. One decided she wasn't hungry; the other "hated" lima beans. With undisguised disgust, both flopped down at the table, planted their elbows defiantly in front of them to symbolize overwhelming boredom, and began to argue as to why one had a larger glass of ice water than the other. I sat silent. Gail reminded them that this was my birthday meal and that we intended the occasion to be a happy one. That brought peace long enough for a brief prayer of thanksgiving.

Nothing went right during the meal. The fiercely debated glass of water was tipped over; there was griping over the "large portion" of lima beans (one tablespoonful); the conversation was studded with tattling, protest, ridicules, and sarcasm. Gail grew progressively more hurt as she saw her carefully planned birthday party slipping from intended joy to actual misery.

A reminder that I had originally chosen to be with the children rather than older friends had no effect. In fact, several references to the fact that this was indeed a birthday party didn't help either. Nothing broke through. All my effective-father principles were useless. I could not alter their moods nor bring the momentum of their feelings under control. Something told me that I should dismiss them both to their rooms, suggesting that they were not fit for proper company, but I kept believing that I could rescue what Gail had worked so hard to produce. But I couldn't!

I suppose the apex of the disaster was reached when both kids finished their meals and suggested that they would like to go back downstairs until we parents finished. "Why don't you call us when it's time for dessert?" they said. "Maybe we can catch the last part of 'The Brady Bunch'."

Normally I would not have permitted them to go. In this case I was just happy to see the poisonous spirit of things depart from the room. When they were gone, Gail and I sat and stared at each other, almost in shock. What had gone wrong? Why were our children so selfish, so insensitive that they hadn't even cared that it was their father's birthday? Why couldn't we control the situation? How could I write a book called *The Effective Father* when I felt so utterly ineffective? Where were the two of them heading in life, we asked, if they could not be more thoughtful than they had been this evening. It was the most miserable birthday I could remember.

Gail rose to clear the table. "I'll get the cake and the presents," she said.

"Oh, no!" I thought. "Ice cream and presents after a family performance like this?"

"Wait," I said. "Let's clear the table, clean the kitchen, sit back and watch what happens. I'm in no mood for festivities after the way the kids behaved. This may be an evening from which we can all learn something."

We followed through on my suggestion and later went to the living room to relax and talk. The evening hours passed. Not a word from the children. "Surely," I thought, "they'll come upstairs at eight to get the party going again." But they didn't! Perhaps at nine? Nine came and went and we could still hear the TV grinding out one program after another.

"Surely you're not going to let them get away with this, are you?" Gail asked. I admitted that I had no idea what should be done. One thing was sure, I remarked. No way could there be a party tonight. The children would have to learn that their selfishness caused sadness for everyone. The lesson would cost their father something.

At 9:30 I called downstairs to the children to come up to bed. They came. "What about the party?" one asked. "Isn't Dad going to open his presents? Aren't we going to eat some cake?"

"No," I replied. "A party happens when people want to show love to one another. A party happens when people are all working together to please the person for whom the party is held. That hasn't happened tonight. So your Mother and I have decided that there will be no party. Perhaps we can have it on another evening when our family shows that it's possible to get along with each other and control ugly feelings."

There was shock. Then there was protest. Finally, tears. Later, I sat at the edge of Kristi's bed and she sobbed out every word that she could think of to express her sorrow and remorse. "Dad, when my birthday comes, let's cancel my party so I can know exactly how you feel tonight. I'm so sorry."

As I rubbed her little back, I could almost feel the rebellion, the mood, the feelings of selfishness draining out of her. When she fell asleep, I could see little trails where tears had streamed down her cheeks.

A few minutes later I talked quietly with Mark as he slowly drifted into drowsiness. Boys don't cry so easily; Mark is no exception. He was silent for many minutes. "Son," I said, "I'm disappointed about the party this evening, of course. But far more disappointing is the fact that it seems to me that you really don't care. Am I reading you correctly? Are you saying to me that it doesn't matter to you that your father's birthday party was ruined?"

Silence!

Then slowly, painfully the response came. "Dad, all evening I sat down in the basement wanting to tell you I was sorry. But I couldn't find the right words. I just couldn't bring myself to do it. I don't know what happened tonight. At the table the nasty words just kept coming out of my mouth. I couldn't get control of myself. I'm really sorry, Dad!"

A few minutes later he was asleep. At his bedside I brood and pray . . .

> How could it be, God,
> That at one moment
> I could confidently express
> What I believe to be
> The principles of genius
> In raising children,
> Of being an effective father?
>
> But at another time
> Fall so utterly impotent
> So as to suspect
> That I know nothing
> That I've done nothing
> That it all amounts to nothing?
>
> After having poured
> The treasures of Heaven
> Into this life of mine,
> Are you often hurt like this?
> Are there strange divine moments
> When you also feel this futility,
> This "powerlessness"

When those called by your
Family name are out of control
And ruin your celebration?

Do you ever share this feeling
That cuts tonight so deeply into my spirit?
If you do,
I, too, am sorry.

I walked out to where Gail sat. The disappointment
and frustration of the evening had left us both drained.
We talked about the evening's frustrating events. We
imagined our children growing older, entering adolescence, gaining their own senses of identity and independence. Would there be many more evenings like this
one? Would the misery of this three-hour time frame be
expanded into days, months, or even years? We had a
feeling of total defeat. Some would say it's only one
evening. But what parent is there who hasn't taken one
single event and, having lost his perspective, felt that this
is typical of the whole process of family life.

As a pastor, I spend many hours with the parents of
adolescent children who are living in prolonged rebellion. If I were to tell them the story of my aborted birthday party, they would smile indulgently and murmur
some version of the saying "You ain't seen nothing yet!"
They would insist that they have endless chains of bizarre stories that could make mine sound insignificant by
contrast. Call them the defeated parents.

Some defeated parents are bitter, disillusioned, and
could be among the over 75 percent of the letter writers
who recently indicated to one of the leading newspaper
columnists that childrearing had been a miserable experience and that, were they to have a new start in life,
they would never repeat the hassle of having a family.

Such bitterness causes them to total up the money invested in education, the energies expended in projects and activities, and call it all a waste. Disillusioned parents smirk at the young adults who have tiny children and drop snide comments such as, "Enjoy them while they're young. They'll crush you later on."

A second class of defeated parents are those who may not be bitter, but simply sad and bewildered. They spend many hours quietly reflecting on where they made the wrong turns. They recall the good days: the days of infancy, the cute stage when nothing could go wrong, the early years when the sky seemed the limit of opportunity. Now, they ask, what happened to our dreams? Were we too strict? Were we too permissive? Which series of events? What decision? Which influences set what seemed to be a beautiful family disastrously off course? Like the instant replay on the TV sports programs, they rehearse the past, wondering how it all fell apart. And each time they die a little bit inside as they see the chasm broaden between their convictions and their children's behavior.

Another group of defeated parents are defiant. They are emphatic in their claims that they have done nothing wrong. If you listen to them defend their methods and motives—"We gave our children the best we had to offer"—you sense that in their harshness is a guarantee that family reconciliation will never take place. If you visit their home, you look in vain for family pictures. The children are never mentioned in the conversation. It is as if any memory of the past is being blotted out.

I have fresh grief for every one of these defeated parents. With the disillusioned, I find myself trying to emphasize the fact that God in his creative activity did not make mistakes—even if sometimes we do. With the saddened, my emphasis is that there is always the hope of

healing and reconciliation. With the defiant, I try lovingly to highlight the fact that there is no innocent party in
a broken relationship.

As a counselor it is not difficult to survey past family
performances and focus in on the mistakes that have
brought children to the point of resenting their parents
and, as a result, often hating their parents' God. Objective hindsight is relatively easy in most cases. One can
point out the enormous amount of hours put in at the
office, building a career at the expense of the family. Or
a finger can be leveled at the number of week-ends away
with friends for hunting and fishing. Add to that the
pursuit of other nonfamily interests night after night. Or
perhaps an uncontrolled temper, an inconsistent disci-
plinary strategy, or a preoccupation with a perfection
that no young person could match is the root cause of
relational disaster. Perhaps I could demonstrate to a father that he was never genuine in his exposure of himself
to his children, that he was really two different persons
depending upon the circumstances and that his children
saw right through it all from the start. I just might be able
to reveal such things.

A father listening to my analysis just might repent,
too. He might see it all in an existential flash and fall to
his knees asking God's forgiveness. He might emerge
from our confrontation a tender man, seeing for the first
time the rigidity or the spinelessness of his former life.
My analysis and his repentance could be a relatively pre-
dictable thing. Naturally! Faced with the consequences
of failure most defeated fathers will do almost anything.
But what is up for grabs is the response of the children.
The chances are that the children will not respond to a
father's remorse or efforts of reconciliation. And that is
the hard part: helping parents see that their children,
now launched into life, must make and be responsible for

their own choices. Those are the moments when I hurt the most: having to comfort a person who has to live with the fruits of his or her past parental performance, helpless to do anything about it.

I tell my friend the physician that I wish I could prescribe a pill that would heal the wounds of the broken people who come to see me. He laughs tolerantly at my jest, but he knows what I mean: there is no instant cure for defeated parents. So instead of pills I search for right words, correct biblical insights, and meaningful prayer requests that may rebuild the spirits of devastated mothers and fathers. I can't ignore the fact, however, that the only authentic comfort would be a guarantee that everything will turn out all right. If their children would come back home from parts unknown, if they would make a commitment to God and launch out on a different style of life, if they would cease filling their lives with destructive tastes, values, and relationships. It sounds good, but such a restoration may not be immediately plausible. What do we do in the meantime?

What comfort can I give in the absence of such total restoration? At best it is a comfort with limits, but I can first affirm God's forgiveness to the defeated mother or father who painfully face their mistakes. Such forgiveness does not obviate the fact that many consequences of past sins will live on. But it does guarantee that they can have a fresh and life-giving rightness with God that they may not have had for a long time, if ever. Life is not over, I say; pieces can be picked up; guilt can be dissolved. While there will be sadness, there can also be new horizons.

A second thrust of comfort I can give to defeated parents is the fact that their children remain under God's care. I can underline the biblical hope that "with God all things are possible."

I open the New Testament to the story of the prodigal son. Here is a classic story of severed relationships. Here is a boy who saw privileges as rights and grabbed every one of them. When he had what he wanted he left home, apparently recognizing no sense of gratitude or responsibility to his father. Here is a father who could have become embittered, hardened, resigned to the fact that in his son's betrayal it was all over and that life had played him a dirty trick. But he didn't.

The Scripture indicates that the defeated father was possessed of a hope. There is a key phrase in the text. "When the boy came to himself. . . . " It simply means that there came a time when in the "famine" of life, the young man did a self-evaluation. His cash flow was nonexistent. His fair-weather friends had deserted him. And the thing he wanted most—his freedom—had eluded him in the crisis moment. Here he was: beholden to an owner of swine, living and eating not like the owner, but like the owner's animals. When he hit bottom he came to himself. The only fixed reality left in his life was his home. With that in mind he started on the way back.

Fortunately, the father had never done or said anything to make the boy feel that he would not be welcomed. A hopeful father had been wise enough not to burn his end of the bridge. When the boy arrived he found his expectant father *waiting*. There were no hints of recrimination, "I-told-you-so," or statements of conditional trust. Just the opposite! There was *healing*.

I remind defeated parents of that story and the hope it can instill in their hearts, but I add that if the hope is to be genuine it must be punctuated with the personal assurance to each other and to God that a homecoming must be marked with unconditional acceptance and forgiveness. I have met indignant fathers who endlessly rehearse their children's past mistakes. Their gripe about the marriage partners a son or daughter has chosen, the immorality practiced, or the failures experienced. I have heard them bitterly tell their children that they are not welcome at home—that home will never again be a resource upon which they can draw. I once even saw a father vow to disown his son.

Such men need to brood on the prodigal's father. He was a shockproof man, never ready to call an end to the relationship. The boy may have left his father; but the father never left the boy. And so I add to my pastoral comfort this personal charge: should your son or daughter ever dishonor you by their behavior, never nail shut the front door of your home. Be ready to open it some day "when they come to themselves." Fathers who wait in an open door may eventually find themselves able to help pick up the shattered pieces of a relationship.

A third source of comfort for defeated parents is that God has an amazing network of his people around the world. Parents estranged from their rebellious children have been astounded by cables, letters, and phone calls coming from far-off places. "Hello, Dad . . . Mom. I'd like to come home. I've met some wonderful people here who have helped me to get my head screwed on right. I've come back to God. Now I want to come back to you."

A student goes off to college and his letters indicate a growing reluctance to be committed to the God of his youth. Parental heartbreak grows as it becomes apparent that the son or daughter is pursuing values and relationships antithetical to the ways of the family. Then one day a different kind of letter arrives. "I've met a Christian friend in my fraternity. He has helped me sort some things out and you won't have to worry any more."

A grown-up child enters into a marriage that parents are sure is headed for disaster. Eight, ten, twelve years pass, and the marriage reels along from one crisis to another. Aging parents look on, helpless, grieving over the suffering through which their son or daughter passes. One day: "Dear Mother and Dad. We've met some new friends and started going to church. We're in a neighborhood Bible study and we're sure you'd like to know that God is in the center of our marriage and family. We've got a long way to go, but it all is beginning to make sense now. It is as if we've just gotten married all over again."

A young girl hitchhiking through Europe ends up at L'Abri. A boy in the military meets a chaplain or someone in the barracks who is part of the Navigator organization. A young man finds himself in a leadership prayer meeting each week at lunch hour in his company. The network of caring Christian people covers the earth and it provides the way back for countless rebellious children. So I affirm the need for constant prayer and intercession that the network will one day operate in the life of a child separated from his parents by his behavior or his resentments.

Finally, when I minister to defeated parents, I suggest that the greatest level of comfort is to prepare themselves for the moment when they will be needed again. If a son or daughter should face divorce, loving parents can stand by with proffered support; if one should get in trouble with the law, it is a time to swallow parental pride and identify. If a child should fail, it is a time to offer a haven for healing. No condemnation; only help.

For some defeated parents the best never happens. They live life with only the most superficial relationship with their grown-up children. And to them I can only say over and over again, accept your children just as they are. Offer friendship, love, and all the companionship which they will receive. Be silent in your judgments; offer advice only when asked. Do not rejoice in failures, but affirm successes. Love, love, love!

None of us has a guarantee that his children will turn out to be all he might wish. Unlike some, I do not believe that the Bible unconditionally promises that if a father does everything right his children will emerge as unqualified successes. In a father/offspring relationship there are at least two parties, both of whom have to make ultimate decisions for themselves. Such decisions cannot be manipulated or coerced. All children have a right, for example, to accept the God of their fathers and they have the corresponding right to reject him. Parents cannot control that choice. They can only create the atmosphere in which sons or daughters make sound judgments. From that point on, the rest is left in God's hands.

Gail and I sit in our living room on my birthday evening. We are tired but relieved that at least at the end of the confrontation an issue was resolved and both Mark and Kristen have learned once again how miserable life becomes for everyone if someone chooses the way of resistance and selfishness. Perhaps tomorrow night will be different. Perhaps there will be a new mood and a new impetus to resume the "rained-out" party. The cake will keep for twenty-four hours; the presents will wait. When we finally get to them it will be in the wake of one further step toward family maturity in which we have all learned what life demands in each of its relationships.

In this late night hour I reflect that I have faced a microcosm of total defeat as a father. The taste is indeed sour, and I muse on how horrible it would be for family affairs to be like this every day of the year. I grimace at such a thought and resolve again that I will work all the harder to be the kind of perceptive and disciplined father that heads rebellion and its consequences off at the pass.

Can I be an effective father by myself? No way! I've already learned many times that I cannot. All the wisdom and sensitivity in the world could not make me an effec-

tive father unless I had a healthy and productive relationship with my wife, Gail. I need her balance, her encouragement, her criticism, and her complementary
feminine contributions to the family. Whoever said it
first was right: my best gift to my children is that of a
happy marriage. The health of my marriage has a direct
relationship to my capacity to be a good father.

I know that I cannot be an effective father without my
church either. I must trust that there are other men and
women with mutual commitments in life who will have
an effect upon my children. They will be those who teach
them in Sunday school, sponsor their youth groups, and
perhaps even counsel them in tight moments in their
growing lives when I will know nothing. As my children
take their place in the fellowship of the church, these
folks will add to the life-way that I've given them and
which they've received from others. Yes, I desperately
need the church and I can see its place in the equation of
effective fatherhood. It cannot be ignored or neglected.

But there is a third force from which effective fatherhood emerges, and it comes from my own healthy relationship to the living God.

One of the most dramatic encounters recorded in the
New Testament happened on the western shores of Lake
Galilee. Emerging from a fishing boat, Jesus Christ
found himself confronted by a man possessed with the
power of total evil. The writer describes this man as a
miserable human being. So bizarre was his antisocial
behavior that his community found it necessary to expel
him. On many nights his friends and family could hear
him running across the countryside, shrieking out in
rage and in terror as he fought for restored peace and
order in his life. He was an embarrassment and inconvenience to everyone. He was nonproductive and ineffective. The only solution to the problem of this man

was to get him out of the sight and responsibility of everyone.

The Bible records that Jesus Christ targeted his divine power upon this pathetic man and his inner being was instantly purged of the horrible and twisted influence which had perverted it. When his family and friends arrived on the scene minutes later, they saw a man "sitting, clothed, and in his right mind." That's first-century language describing a person whose life has been reordered and renewed. And what did Jesus tell this healed man to do? Travel with him? No! Go to seminary and study for religious ministry? Wrong again! His command was simple and direct: "Go home! Tell your friends what the Lord has done for you."

The effective father is, above all things, a man touched by the power of Jesus Christ. The Bible teaches that there comes a time in every life when a person must make a most important decision: what to do about God, his Maker. That's where Christ enters the picture, for he is the one who introduces us and makes our relationship with God healthy and whole. During Christ's public ministry, men of all kinds had to decide where they stood in relationship with him. Some rejected him and went their way. Others followed him and their lives changed. For most, the change was a process of maturing, and each day they learned more about Christ and his way of life and gained increasing mastery over their instincts, emotions, and intellects. The results of these changes were very practical—and that's why I mention the deranged man at the shore. He's typical of others whom Christ sent home. Home is where life is lived. Home is where one's children are shaped and sculpted. Jesus liberated this man not to become a great religious personality, but simply to go home where he belonged and to do his daily work.

"Going home" symbolizes everything there is to me

about productive relationships. That's where I am known most intimately and have my greatest potential effectiveness as a human being. It is the power of Jesus Christ, therefore, that makes me capable of carrying out all the principles I have mentioned. It is he who, having changed my life and started me on the process of daily spiritual maturity, sends me home to be an effective father. Without him I cannot find the energy I need to implement the principles of effective fatherhood.

No man who reads this book may ever be in as much spiritual hot water as the demon-possessed man at the lake. But many men may have the same basic need: the power of Jesus Christ to reorder their priorities, renew their energies, and refresh their capacities. To such men I candidly urge a prayer of introduction to Jesus who waits for any of us to address him by name and share our need for a relationship with God. The Bible affirms his desire to respond.

Gail and I look at each other after many moments of silence in which we have been thinking similar thoughts, and we finally agree about the lateness of the hour, the fatigue in our bodies, and the fact that as a father and mother we've done everything there is to do in this day. As I head down the hallway to our bedroom, I make one final check in each child's room. And as I close their doors, assured that all is well, I find myself praying all the harder, "Lord, above all the things you allow me to be and to do, make me a good husband and an effective father. By contrast, nothing else counts."

NOTES

1. From *Newsweek* magazine, September 25, 1972. Copyright 1972 by Newsweek, Inc. All rights reserved. Reprinted by permission.

2. From "The Shaping," by Dale Martin Stone. As quoted in *The Disciplines of Life*, by V. Raymond Edman, Victor Books, 1948.

3. From the *Pennsylvania State Law Enforcement Journal*. As quoted in Robert Raines, *Creative Brooding*, Macmillan, 1966.

4. From the *Stanford Observer*. As quoted in *Wittenburg Door*.

5. From *The One and Only You*, Bruce Larson. Copyright 1974, Word Books, Waco, Texas. Used by permission.

6. From the song "Cat's in the Cradle" written by Sandy Chapin and Harry Chapin, © 1974 Story Songs Ltd. (ASCAP). Used by permission. All rights reserved.